Memories of
Times Past

Nebraska painters and paperhangers boast of their product's white lead content.

A young family shares an afternoon snack.

An Iowa farmer delivers his daily gathering of eggs, to be sold for fifty-seven cents a dozen.

MEMORIES OF
Times Past

Young photographers pose with their then-modern cameras in the early twentieth century.

IDEALS PUBLICATIONS
NASHVILLE, TENNESSEE

ISBN 0-8249-5855-1

Published by Ideals Publications, a division of Guideposts
535 Metroplex Drive, Suite 250
Nashville, Tennessee 37211
www.idealsbooks.com

Color separations by Precision Color Graphics, Franklin, Wisconsin
Printed and bound in Italy

Library of Congress CIP data on file

10 9 8 7 6 5 4 3 2 1

Publisher, Patricia A. Pingry
Associate Publisher, Peggy Schaefer
Editor, Michelle Prater Burke
Book Designer, Eve DeGrie
Production Artist, Marisa Calvin

Cover photograph, Ideals Publications

ACKNOWLEDGMENTS

Baker, Russell. Excerpt from *Growing Up*, copyright © 1982 by Russell Baker. Reprinted by permission of NTC Contemporary Publishing Co. Cantwell, Mary. Excerpt from *American Girl*, copyright © 1992 by Mary Cantwell. Used by permission of Random House, Inc. Carroll, Gladys Hasty. Excerpt from *To Remember Forever*, copyright © 1963 by Gladys Hasty Carroll. Reprinted by permission of Little, Brown, and Co., Inc. Cather, Willa. Excerpt from *The Bohemian Girl*. Reprinted from *Willa Cather's Collected Short Fiction*, 1892–1912 edited by Virginia Faulkner by permission of the University of Nebraska Press. Copyright © 1965, 1970 by the University of Nebraska Press. Copyright © renewed 1993, 1998 by the University of Nebraska Press. Gilbreth, Frank B., Jr. Excerpt from *Time Out for Happiness*, copyright © 1970 by Frank B. Gilbreth, Jr. Reprinted by permission of HarperCollins Publishers, Inc. Holmes, Marjorie. "A Lizzie, My Love and You" and "Give Me an Old-Fashioned Peddler" from *You and I and Yesterday*. Reprinted by permission of the author. Jaques, Edna. "The School" and "The Picnic to the Hills" from *Uphill All the Way* and "Prairie Born" from *Aunt Hattie's Place*. Used by permission of Thomas Allen & Son Limited, Canada. Lehrer, Jim. Excerpt from *A Bus of My Own*, copyright © 1992 by Jim Lehrer. Reprinted by permission of Putnam Publishing Group. McCullers, Carson. "Home for Christmas" from *The Mortgaged Heart* by Carson McCullers, Copyright © 1940, 1941, 1942, 1945, 1949, 1953, 1956, 1959, 1963, 1967, 1971 by Floria V. Lasky, Executrix of the Estate of Carson McCullers. Reprinted by permission of Houghton Mifflin Co. All Rights Reserved. McGinnis, R. J. "The Family Cow" and "The Country Doctor" from *The Good Old Days*, copyright © 1960 by F & W

Publications Corp. Used by permission of Fitzhenry & Whiteside Limited. Rich, Louise Dickinson. "How Firm a Foundation" and "Home Town" from *Innocence Under the Elms*, copyright © 1955 by Louise Dickinson Rich. Used by permission of the author's estate and Curtis Brown Ltd. "Christmas in the Woods" from *We Took to the Woods*, copyright © 1942, renewed 1970 by Louise Dickinson Rich. Reprinted by permission of HarperCollins Publishers, Inc. Strong, Patience. "Nostalgia." Reprinted by permission of Rupert Crew Limited. Stuart, Jesse. Excerpt from *A Jesse Stuart Reader* selected and introduced by Jesse Stuart. Copyright ©1963 by McGraw-Hill Book Company. Copyright © renewed 1991 by Jesse Stuart Foundation. Used by permission of Jesse Stuart Foundation, P.O. Box 391, Ashland, KY 41114. Taber, Gladys. Excerpt from *Especially Father*, copyright © 1948 by the Curtis Publishing Co., copyright © 1949 by Gladys Taber, copyright renewed 1975, 1976 by Gladys Taber. All rights reserved. Reprinted by permission of Brandt and Brandt Literary Agents, Inc. White, E. B. Excerpt from "Farewell, My Lovely!" from *Essays of E. B. White* (Harper and Row). Copyright © 1936 by The New Yorker Magazine, Inc. Originally published in *The New Yorker* in 1936 over the pseudonym "Lee Strout White." Richard L. Strout had submitted a manuscript on the Ford, and White, with his collaboration, rewrote it. Excerpt from "The Railroad" from *Essays of E. B. White* (Harper and Row). Reprinted by permission; copyright © 1960 E. B. White. Originally in *The New Yorker*. All rights reserved. Young, Carrie. "North Dakota Cook," originally appearing as "A Scandinavian Thanksgiving in North Dakota" in *Gourmet*, copyright © 1983 by Gourmet, reprinted by permission.

TABLE OF CONTENTS

CHAPTER ONE
Parks, Parades, and Penny Candy:
MEMORIES OF MAIN STREET
6

CHAPTER TWO
A Fence, a Farm, and a Family Cow:
MEMORIES OF THE COUNTRY
44

CHAPTER THREE
Trips, Trains, and a Model T:
MEMORIES OF GOING PLACES
82

CHAPTER FOUR
Family, Friends, and the Front-Porch Swing:
MEMORIES OF HOME
114

INDEX
160

Parks, Parades, and Penny Candy:
MEMORIES OF MAIN STREET

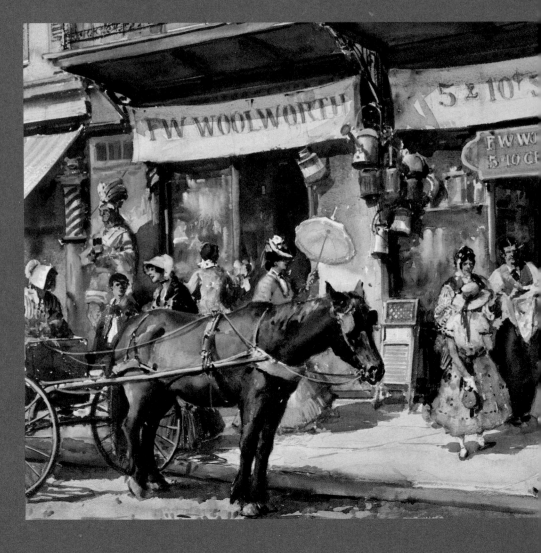

Remember a Town

I remember a town and a pleasant street
Where the maple trees flung high
Their shading branches through summer days
Beneath a calm blue sky.

I remember the children who ran and played
On corners beneath the lights;
Their shrill young voices gay and sweet
Those quiet starlit nights.

I shall always remember the popcorn man
And the concerts in the square;
Kindly faces of those I loved;
Almost I see them there.

I remember a man with warm brown eyes
In a little grocery store,
Who for my penny always gave
Six chocolates, sometimes more.

I remember a town though the years are long
And miles lie in between;
A town that is dearest to my heart
Of all the towns I've seen.

Sheila Stinson

Shoppers enjoy the wares at the corner store in artist James Sessions'
painting In Front of an F. W. Woolworth 5 & 10 Cent Store.

HOME TOWN

Louise Dickinson Rich

*T*he fact that Central Square was really not a square but a long, slightly elliptic rectangle didn't disturb me at all, so complete was my acceptance of the established world. It couldn't very well be square, because then there wouldn't be room for the Academy building, the Town Hall, and the Swedenborgian and Congregational churches at the south end; or else the Bridgewater Inn, A.I. Simmons' Market, Casey's Ice Cream Parlor, and the watering trough at the foot of the Common would have to be lopped off the north. Central Square obviously had to be the way it was. . . .

All the grocery stores sold penny candy, but we favored Alden's for reasons that were sound and compelling to us, irrelevant as they might appear to adult logic. None of these reasons had to do with the quality or assortment of the candy, which varied not at all from store to store. Alden's was not the largest grocery store, or the most convenient, but the horse that hauled their delivery wagon all over town was a personal friend of ours, a big, amiable gray with a mind of his own, so that if he thought the delivery man was spending too much time in the kitchen of a customer, he'd unassumingly take matters unto his own cognizance and amble along to the next regular stop. We felt that it would be disloyal to him to patronize any other store. In addition, Alden's displayed a life-size Fairy Soap poster, showing the picture of a little girl with long curls, and demanding searchingly, "Have you a little fairy in *your* home?" This was at once our joy and our despair. We'd stand there in our homemade, plain and practical dresses with our straight hair skinned back in tight, neat braids—by no stretch of the imagination could the most astigmatic mistake us for little fairies out of anybody's home—

> *The fact that Central Square was really not a square . . . didn't disturb me at all.*

and wish that we looked exactly like that little girl, and that we had fur-trimmed coats and bonnets just like hers.

Then too, Alden's had a peanut butter machine, a marvel of modernity. At the other stores, peanut butter was dipped in the required amounts out of tubs into cardboard containers. If you were smart, you transferred it to a glass jar as soon as you got it home, because the oil separated from the solid peanut particles and oozed through the cardboard all over the place; and you stored the jar upside down to encourage a more even texture to the spread, although this gambit was never entirely successful. Even Alden's marvelous machine did not have the answer to this technical difficulty, which today's manufacturers seem to have overcome; but the gourmets of the peanut butter world maintained that there was no comparison possible between the ordinary tub butter and that which came fresh out of Alden's revolutionary machine, a simple red-and-gold-painted grinder into the top of which went whole peanuts and salt, and out of the bottom of which, when the clerk turned the hand crank, came the peanut butter in a rather revolting manner. We didn't think so then, though. We thought the whole thing

made our difficult choices, coping with the complicated mathematics involved with no sign of any other emotion than sympathetic helpfulness. There were no candy bars in those days. Adults bought boxes of chocolates sometimes, on very special occasions.

After taking a customer's choices off the shelves, a grocer records her purchases.

was fascinating; and moreover, once in a while we were allowed to help ourselves to a cracker out of the barrel, scrape the residue of peanut butter from the machine's vent, and eat it. It tasted ambrosial, much better than the same thing did at home. . . .

And last, Tom Alden always had all the time in the world for us. He must have known perfectly well that our top spending power never exceeded four cents, and yet no matter who was waiting to be served, he'd stand relaxed and patient and courteous while we

Children bought penny candy: "liquorish" shoe strings, candy cigarettes, large semi-translucent pink or white peppermints, candy pipes, candy pebbles that looked real, candy corn that did not, and little foil pie-plates full of sweet goo and accompanied by Lilliputian spoons, fine for doll's teas. Then there were bright red cinnamon drops that bit the tongue, and lollipops with poisonous-looking green or red bull's eyes in the centers, and big sticks of OK gum in red

A soda shop of the past sports a tin ceiling and shiny serving pieces.

any of this kind here; or two of these *and* one of these. He'd count them carefully into the small paper bag, gay with green and pink and purple pinstripes against its unbleached beige surface. I don't know why he bothered. . . . Perhaps he was simply representative of a more leisurely era. At any rate, he certainly was nice to all children. . . .

The stores were wonderful places, rich and bountiful. Cream of Wheat came in packages, and so did Quaker Oats and confectioner's sugar, but almost nothing else did. Brown sugar, full of

wrappers, and hoarhound lozenges, and striped peppermint sticks, and candy ice-cream cones, and a dozen other strange and wonderful confections.

Some things were a cent apiece, but only the foolish and improvident invested in those, or in soft candies that were gone in a gulp. Alice and I worked too hard for our money to fritter it away like that. We chose the more-for-a-penny kinds, and Tom Alden let us split up our purchase: one of these at ten for a penny leaves nine tenths of a cent, minus two of these at five for a penny leaves you half a cent. These are two for a penny; you could have one of these; or five of

delicious lumps that melted exquisitely on the tongue, and flour and crackers and dill pickles and walnuts stood about in barrels. Huge whole cheeses, from which the clerk would cut a sliver so you could try before buying, and wicker baskets of eggs rested on the counters. There were two tubs of butter, creamery and dairy, from which a really good clerk could cut a pound block to the fraction of an ounce on the first try. Cookies didn't come pre-packaged, but were weighed out of glass-fronted boxes into the brass scoop of a balance scale. I can see the hand of the grocer yet, poised, full of gingersnaps, over the scales as he debated with himself the dropping of the one more that would bring it a hair over the pound or just letting it ride as it was. And there was a type of Nabisco colored and shaped like a paper-shelled almond and filled with a firm, pale fondant. My idea of the ultimate bliss was that one day I would be able to buy absolutely all of those that I could eat. But of course I never had enough money for that; and now that I could possibly, if pressed, scrape up the cash, I never see them any more. That's Life; and no doubt it's better so. Without doubt they'd have lost the heavenly flavor they used to have.

Coffee beans roasted to deepening shades of brown stood in galvanized buckets on the floor along the counter in those days, and you selected the roast you preferred, either to be ground on the spot in the hand-operated grinder, or taken home to be ground as you used it in your own square little wooden grinder with the drawer that pulled out at the bottom. All the stores always smelled of fresh-ground coffee and of the kerosene which spilled, in spite of the potato that the clerk took out of the barrel and stuck firmly onto the spout of the gallon can you'd brought to be filled. . . .

Fall was the time of year when Central Square came to life. Hayes' salted peanuts were a fall and winter feature. Mr. Hayes, who ran one of the ice cream parlors, roasted and salted them himself every day, taking them out of the oven in the late forenoon. There were never any peanuts like them anywhere, and people made a point of stopping in to get them while

The stores were wonderful places, rich and bountiful.

they were still hot. He kept them in an enormous age-crazed cream-and-rose china bowl, bigger than the biggest punch bowl, on the front corner of the soda fountain, with a teacup alongside; and for a nickel you could buy a cup full to overflowing. Nobody'd dream of buying peanuts anywhere except at Hayes'.

Casey's was the place to go for a sundae in the afternoon, although you might go to Hayes' at any other time of day. Hayes' had round tables with wire legs, and wire chairs, and they served saltines with their ice cream.

Who could resist Mr. Brown's famous popcorn at two bags for a nickel?

But Casey's was really elegant. They had square tables with attached stools which swung out on arms to accommodate the sitter, and the parlor was separated from the less genteel transactions of the store proper by a bead curtain, which struck my sister and me, on the rare occasions when some well-heeled relative treated us there, dumb with admiration, so that we found it difficult—but not impossible—to indicate our choice of sustenance. We always had the same thing, the nut-fudge-marshmallow special, covered with chocolate shot and topped by a maraschino cherry. Casey's fudge sauce—well, we swooned at the thought of it. It was hot and darkly thick, and congealed to a gummy consistency around the cone of vanilla ice cream. An effete detail of Casey's service was the silver (simulated, I'm sure) dish with paper liner in which the sundae was presented. We discovered early that we could take the liner out, flatten it to a disc on the table top, and scrape off the last, lingering, delicious trace of the sauce, which otherwise might have been criminally wasted. We didn't get behind Casey's bead curtain often, but when we did, we made the most of it.

There was more to the town than just the Square and the stores around it, though; much, much more. There was the street on which we lived and the immediately adjacent streets to which our mother limited our unsupervised roamings—or thought that she did. We should have felt restricted, but ordinarily we didn't. The world has never seemed as big and various since as it did then, when it was bounded by a few blocks. . . .

Those were the limits of our experience and our rovings, and they were wide enough. Everything that could have happened to us anywhere—joy and grief, gain and loss, contentment and furious revolt, all of the things we were to encounter in greater or lesser degree up to the days of our deaths—happened to us within these boundaries.

The Candy Store

A licorice whip or jelly bean
Transports me to a bygone scene,
Where once I stood with hungry eyes,
And murmured little yearning sighs
For gingerbread and lemon drops
And chicken corn and lollipops.

For there I'd stand in mute despair,
An indecisive millionaire,
With fifty ways I might disburse
The two whole pennies in my purse.

So teetering from toe to heel,
I'd wheedle me a special "deal"
For one of those and two of this,
A jujube and a taffy kiss,
A sour ball, a slice of gum,
A hoarhound drop, a sugar plum.

The flight of memory takes me back
To the penny candy in the striped paper sack.

Phyllis I. Rosenteur

The Sidewalks of New York

CHAS. MILLER

CHAS. B. LAWLOR AND JAMES W. BLAKE

1. Down in front of Ca-sey's_____ Old brown wood - en stoop,_____ On a sum - mer's eve-ning, We formed a mer - ry group;_____ Boys and girls to - geth-er, We would sing and waltz,_____ While the "Gin - nie" played the or - gan On the____ side-walks of New York.

2. That's where John - ny Ca - sey_____ And lit - tle Jim - my Crowe, With Ja - key Krause the ba - ker, Who al - ways had the dough;_____ Pret - ty Nel - lie Shan-non With a dude as light as cork, First picked up the waltz step On the____ side-walks of New York.

3. Things have changed since those times,_____ Some are up in "g"_____ Oth - ers they are wand - 'rers. But they all feel just like me;_____ They would part with all they've got, Could they but once more walk, With their best girl and have a twirl, On the side-walks of New York.

"East side, West side, All around the town. . ."

East   side,   West   side,   All   a - round   the

town,_____   The   tots   sang "ring___ a ro - sie,"   "Lon - don

Bridge is   fall - ing down;"_____   Boys   and   girls   to -

geth-er,_____   Me   and   Ma - mie Rorke,_____   Tripped   the

light   fan - tas-tic,   On   the   side-walks   of   New York._____

In a Little World These Men Stood Tall

Catherine Otten

O urs was a house divided. At the turn of the century, our family moved into our brand-new house, which was divided into a grocery store in the front, and our home in the back and above the store. It stood on a corner of the city limits and it soon became the center of all neighborhood activities.

Being the children of a storekeeper had its advantages. Everyone for blocks around knew us. There was no generation gap in those days. Other children were not our only friends. Customers as well as the salesmen and peddlers who called at our store and worked in the neighborhood were also our friends. There was the milkman, the fruitman, the candyman, the iceman, the ragman, the lamplighter, and the policeman.

The best grown-up friend a child had in the neighborhood was the policeman who walked our beat. . . .

Immaculately clean and polished, he "reported in" each morning from the police box on our corner. It was a six-sided, grayish-blue structure which occupied only about three square feet. It contained a telephone and a couple of hooks for the policeman's rain gear. Occasionally, our friend the policeman would gather a bunch of giggling kids and lock them up in his fascinating little police box. "We got arrested today," they would brag to their families when they returned home.

The duties and responsibilities of a policeman those days were simple. Sometimes for weeks, his chief business was watching for broken boards in our wooden sidewalks as he walked his beat. Finding lost children and pets, looking in on dance halls and saloons to spot any violations were duties that seldom taxed his endurance. Mediating family squabbles and misbehaviors was also part of his responsibility. Our policeman knew every family on his beat, and he was a friend to all of them.

Perhaps the best-loved man in the lives of a storekeeper's children was the candyman. He arrived weekly in his pretty, horse-drawn wagon with all the pomp and flourish of a circus entertainer. He expected an eager gathering of young admirers, and he was seldom disappointed. Because we were the kids who lived in the store, we could follow this happy, pudgy, white-haired little man into the store. The rest of the kids had to be content with pressing their noses to the window.

Our candyman was as sweet and good as his merchandise. Sometimes he would consult one of us kids about the merit of some new candy novelty if Mama hesitated to order. I remember well the day he let me choose a little wax bottle of colored syrup for each of my friends outside. The samples paid off. Demand made reordering necessary over and over again. The sweetened wax bottles were drained and then chewed like gum for a long time after.

Some of the candies were "seasonal specials." As Easter drew near, the box of chocolate marshmallow eggs tempted the "gamblers," young and old alike. A customer chose his own egg from the box, and bit into it. If the egg had a pink center he could choose another one free. Of course, he bit into that one too, hoping to find another pink center. The one day that always sold out on "specials" was April Fool's Day. Children saved their pennies for weeks so they could treat their friends . . .

"Here comes the iceman" was a familiar chant heard in the neighborhood on hot summer days. The iceman, like the policeman, belonged to the neighborhood. The grocery store, the butcher shop and the saloon were his biggest customers, but almost every house also had an icebox in those days.

Like the milkman, the iceman made his rounds, and like the candyman, he had his followers. There was always a thirsty group of kids watching anxiously as he chipped away on the huge blocks of ice. In noisy admiration, they would cheer as he caught up the heavy cold block with his iron tongs, hurled it over

his shoulder, and lugged it to the waiting wooden icebox. While he was gone, of course, the kids helped themselves to the icy chips, and sucked away in pure delight.

On scorching hot summer days, his group of freeloaders resembled a little parade, and it lasted until the last block of ice was delivered. Then the iceman, with a generous flourish, would brush the sawdust-covered leftover pieces of melting ice out onto the road for the big scramble.

Gus, the lamplighter, was a daily visitor in the neighborhood. Some child often made the rounds "helping" him light up the corner gas lamps. Gus was a big, rough, happy fellow who came twice a day; early in the morning to put out the high lights with his long hooked pole, and again late in the afternoon to turn them on again.

Gus limped painfully, so it was not hard for the children to keep up with him as he did his "magic tricks" at each stop. He spoke only German, so even if he tried to explain it remained a mystery to his young fans.

Every now and then the waffleman came around. He announced his arrival by blowing a little trumpet, and that was the only invitation necessary. By the time the waffle wagon got to your house, you were out waiting to spend a nickel for a big, brown, powdered-sugared treat.

The iceman, the waffleman, and the lamplighter no longer exist. Progress has taken them out of the picture. But the memories of them are tucked away in my heart and in the hearts of many others of my generation. They are marked, "Childhood Memories—fragile, handle with care."

A small-town church awaits its Sunday churchgoers.

The Little Church

The little church of Long Ago, where as a boy I sat
With mother in the family pew, and fumbled with my hat—
How I would like to see it now the way I saw it then,
The straight-backed pews, the pulpit high, the women and the men
Dressed stiffly in their Sunday clothes and solemnly devout,
Who closed their eyes when prayers were said and never looked about—
That little church of Long Ago, it wasn't grand to see,
But even as a little boy it meant a lot to me.

The choir loft where father sang comes back to me again;
I hear his tenor voice once more the way I heard it when
The deacons used to pass the plate, and once again I see
The people fumbling for their coins, as glad as they could be
To drop their quarters on the plate, and I'm a boy once more
With my two pennies in my fist that mother gave before
We left the house, and once again I'm reaching out to try
To drop them on the plate before the deacon passes by.

It seems to me I'm sitting in that high-backed pew, the while
The minister is preaching in that good old-fashioned style;
And though I couldn't understand it all somehow I know
The Bible was the text book in that church of Long Ago;
He didn't preach on politics, but used the word of God,
And even now I seem to see the people gravely nod,
As though agreeing thoroughly with all he had to say,
And then I see them thanking him before they go away.

The little church of Long Ago was not a structure huge,
It had no hired singers or no other subterfuge
To get the people to attend, 'twas just a simple place
Where every Sunday we were told about God's saving grace;
No men of wealth were gathered there to help it with a gift;
The only worldly thing it had—a mortgage hard to lift.
And somehow, dreaming here to-day, I wish that I could know
The joy of once more sitting in that church of Long Ago.

Edgar A. Guest

OLD-TIME RELIGION

Gone are the days when Sunday mornings meant putting on your best clothes and listening to a lengthy sermon, fan in hand, before heading home to prepare lunch for the preacher. Church socials meant innocent flirtation between youngsters, summers always brought enthusiastic tent revivals complete with spirited traveling evangelists, and evenings year-round were spent reading the Bible together as a family.

A group of Sunday School teachers meeting on the shores of Lake Chautauqua in New York in 1874 were surprised when people by the thousands began joining their lectures and hymn singing. The next summer, the organizers of the first meeting expanded their camp, and what started as four tents on the lakeshore became chalet-style cottages filled with church-group campers discussing and learning everything from religion to social reform.

It was John Wesley, the founder of Methodism, who started the "circuit riding" tradition. For more than fifty years, he travelled on horseback from town to town, preaching sermons at each stop. The tradition continued into the nineteenth century with evangelists such as circuit preacher Peter Cartwright. Meeting houses were few, so Cartwright spoke wherever people would open their homes. Owning only a broadcloth suit, a horse with saddlebags, and his Bible and hymnal, he traveled across the country and preached more than fifteen thousand sermons. Circuit riders such as Cartwright helped plant the seeds of religion across the frontier and offered many isolated communities their only link to evangelism.

One night in 1898, two young salesmen, John Nicholson and Samuel Hill, were asked to share a room when their hotel in Boscobel, Wisconsin, was overbooked. When one of the two men asked to keep the lamp lit to read from the Bible, he discovered the other was a Christian as well, and a lasting friendship began. Nicholson and Hill soon founded a society, named after the Old Testament leader Gideon, with the mission of placing Bibles in hotel rooms across the country. In 1908, the first twenty-five King James Versions were delivered to the Superior Hotel in Iron Mountain, Montana, by Gideon evangelists. Today, Gideon Bibles number more than thirty-two million.

In the early part of the twentieth century, well-known evangelists such as Billy Sunday, a former professional baseball player, spoke to throngs of eager crowds. By his death in 1935, Sunday had preached to millions during more than two hundred campaigns held in tents and temporary wooden structures across the country. It is estimated that three hundred thousand men and women became Christians after hearing Sunday preach and walking down a sawdust-covered aisle to shake his hand.

The old-fashioned outdoor revivals were once a staple of the summer. Permanent meeting structures were often unavailable, so tents or the open air would serve as the only shelter. A guest preacher was brought in for the sometimes week-long event, and singing was sure to be featured prominently. Attendees, many of whom were first-time churchgoers, rode in on horse and buggy and braved the heat to support the tireless preacher with enthusiastic "Amens."

How Firm a Foundation

Louise Dickinson Rich

*T*here used to be a special quality to Sunday mornings that vanished with the common possession of automobiles. . . . Everybody walked to church. So the streets were empty of wheeled traffic, and the whole town seemed to be sleeping in the sun, except for the circumspect church-bound pedestrians strung along the shady sidewalks. Nobody ran or shouted or even walked very fast. Everybody looked dressed up and strange as we joined the crowd converging on our own church and climbed the stairway to the auditorium.

There was nothing of the theatrical about the form of worship of New England Congregationalists. No appeal whatsoever was made to the senses or the emotions. Both the service and the place in which it was held were marked by a restraint and austerity almost monkish. The auditorium was a vast white room of utmost architectural simplicity, with tall windows on both sides and the pews curving around slightly to face the pulpit and choir loft. It was a light and airy place in which the only color was supplied by two commemorative stained-glass windows near the front that threw lozenges of brilliant red and blue and golden light across the painted pew-backs, and a great arrangement of seasonal flowers or potted plants on the table below the pulpit. The pews were straight and narrow and hard, with racks for the hymn books and little holders for the wineglasses on Communion Sunday attached to their backs.

We'd tiptoe down the aisle to our own pew, subdued by the great space around us, and the solemn faces of those already present, and the soft and sonorous playing of the organ, in established order. The usher went first—

The stained-glass windows threw lozenges of brilliant red and blue across the painted pew-backs.

although why I don't know, since we all knew and had known for years where our pew was. Then came my father, then Alice and me, and last my mother, to keep an eye on us. She needn't have bothered. We knew what was expected of us. . . . We were allowed to sit side-by-side as long as we behaved ourselves. If we didn't, at some point in the service our mother would change places with Alice, putting herself between us. When that happened, it boded ill for us after we got home, so we tried to avoid the necessity if possible. After our father had taken his proper place as head of the family at the end of the pew, the usher handed us each a copy of the church calendar, and silently withdrew to the back of the room. . . .

The first part of the service we could endure, even the long prayer in which the minister called to the attention of the Lord any imperfections in the world at home and abroad that He might have over-looked. We didn't listen, of course. But it came early enough in the order of wor-ship so that we hadn't yet developed aches in our backs, cramps in our legs, or a numbness in our derrieres; and we hadn't yet exhausted the feeble entertain-ment possibilities of any funny-looking hats in front of us. Once during the prayer we saw a ladybug crawling over the collar of the dress of the woman in the next pew forward. We watched, fascinated, putting up prayers of our own for it to go down her neck. Just as it seemed as though we had the Lord's Ear, the woman behind us leaned forward and asked our mother in a piercing whisper, well laced with horror, that penetrated to the furthermost ends of the church, "Is it a *bedbug*?" (Silly old hen didn't know a ladybug when she saw one! . . .) That day our mother took the unprecedented step of separating Alice and me right in the mid-dle of the prayer. In spite of the repercussions that followed later, we always hoped that some-thing like that would happen again.

The taking of the collection wasn't so bad, because maybe an usher would drop his plate and have to scramble for the money. No one ever did, but the possibility was present. The

The morning sun brightens a small church in Nova Scotia.

Scripture reading we rather liked (speaking always comparatively), because of the majestic surge of the King James Version, which fell impressively on our language-susceptible ears; and the Responsive Reading was all right, too. The congregation stood during that part, and that gave us a chance to stretch our legs. We could join in the reading, too; although once I became so interested in the text that I went right on reading aloud into the minister's verse, and was so embarrassed that I thought I'd fall down dead. The solos and anthems by the choir were tolerable, since the members made peculiar faces when they reached for notes at the limits of their various ranges, lifting their chins for the high ones and tucking them down into their col-lars for the low. It made a mild diversion.

But the singing of the hymns we really liked, and not only because we again had a chance to stretch our legs and ease our backs, nor because we could participate. Over and above all that, we really loved some of the hymns for themselves. . . . They were ancient

Dressed in their Sunday best, a group of ladies gather outside following the church supper.

for thought during the coming week, and all in all instructive, cultural, uplifting, erudite, and doctrinally sound. That's what they got, too, believe me; and believe me, also, it was all away and gone over Alice's and my heads.

We sat there in the acute agony that only marrow-deep boredom can bring to the very young. We squirmed until our mother laid a restraining hand on the nearest knee. We slumped onto the middles of our spines, rested our heads on the hard back of the pew, and stared at the ceiling until a maternal nudge brought us upright. We scratched ourselves. We read hymns and the Responsive Readings in the back of the hymnal to ourselves, and our Bibles and quarterlies. We counted the number of men in the church and the number of women, and the number of hats with yellow on them, and the number of coats with braid trimming. We counted the number of times *and* was used on the calendar, and the number of words beginning with *h*, and the number of capital letters. We played "Rich man, poor man, beggarman, thief" on the back buttons of dresses in front of us. We yawned and we sighed deeply, and our mother looked at us with pained disapproval. Finally we lapsed into comas and just sat there with our eyes glazed and our mouths slightly ajar, so that when the minister went into the last stretch and came to a triumphant close, he usually took us by surprise. We'd pull ourselves together, join in the last hymn, and in somewhat of a daze, as though coming out from under the effects of a powerful drug, make our way out of the auditorium and down the stairs. . . .

and familiar and full of beautiful phrases that even if not completely understood, gratified some feeling deep within. What we felt, I'm afraid, had nothing to do with religion; although maybe it did, at that. Maybe sincere and involuntary response to any form of religious expression is in itself the beginning of a religious experience.

After the singing of the next-to-the-last hymn came the really tough part of the service. According to the calendar, we were almost to the end. There were just the closing hymn and the benediction to go—*and* the sermon. . . . The congregation expected a solid discourse with points plainly labeled from *firstly* up as high as *seventhly* or *eighthly*, based on a good orthodox text, adorned with classical and Biblical allusions, illustrated with examples from both sacred and profane literature, enlivened perhaps by lessons from real life, containing food

Church activity was not confined to Sunday by any means. There were weekday meetings of the various organizations like the Sewing Circle or Christian Endeavor Society; and every winter there was a big church sale and supper, when everybody pitched in and helped. I don't suppose these were riotous affairs, but they seemed very gala indeed to Alice and me. . . .

Throughout the year there were occasionally the traditional baked bean, cold ham, and potato salad suppers; but the supper that followed the sale was an all-out effort . . . . You paid a flat rate for the supper, and that meant all that you could eat. Seconds on everything were standard, thirds common, and fourths not unknown. The choosing of your pieces of pie and cake was a nerve-racking business. Even the most sanguine couldn't hope to sample them all. The human stomach does have its limits of expansion. But every woman who had been solicited for a dessert had quite naturally put her best foot as far forward as it would go, sparing neither the butter nor the eggs. There was one dark, rich chocolate cake with a thick, buttery mocha frosting—but why torture myself at this late date?

The hot roast lamb supper I remember particularly, since it was the subject of a long and stubborn altercation. Our mother served on the supper committee that year. . . . She'd spend the whole day of the supper at the church and attend all the committee meetings faithfully; and because she didn't have anyone to leave us with and we were too small to be left alone, she took us along with her. We understood that we were to be quiet and good and keep out from underfoot; and we obeyed instructions. We found that it paid. End pieces of cake came our way, pieces that were slightly crumbly or unevenly iced; and if the first cutting out of a pie looked ragged, we were apt to get that, too. We fared very well, and we also had the pleasantly important sensation of knowing what went on behind the scenes, of being In The Know. *We* knew—although we wouldn't have breathed it outside for anything, having great senses of honor and pride in being good security risks—that Mrs. Blank's cakes never appeared on the supper tables at all, because she used a vegetable shortening in place of real butter, and the committee ladies wouldn't put the Congregational reputation in jeopardy by serving them to the general public; and that Mrs. Hunt's white walnut cake made only a token appearance, since it was so wonderful that most of it was eaten in the kitchen. We knew a lot that we didn't tell.

The goods at the local church's bake sale may have resembled these homemade and home-canned treats.

AN OLD-FASHIONED BAKE SALE

The morning of the big bake sale, kitchens across town were filled with the aroma of bread rising and pies baking. Whether the profits from the sale were to go to the community church or the local elementary school, the best cooks in the county were always eager to show off their prized family recipes, and the customers were more than willing to sample the delicious merchandise.

❖ LEMON ICEBOX PIE   (Makes one 9-inch pie)

1¼ cups graham cracker crumbs
¼ cup granulated sugar
¼ cup butter, melted
 1 14-ounce can sweetened condensed milk
 1 6-ounce can frozen lemonade concentrate

1 tablespoon grated lemon peel
1 4-ounce carton frozen whipped topping
  Additional whipped topping
  Thin lemon slices

Preheat oven to 350° F. In a medium bowl, combine crumbs, sugar, and melted butter; mix thoroughly with a fork. Press mixture into the bottom and up the sides of a 9-inch pie plate. Bake 8 to 10 minutes. Cool. In a large mixing bowl, combine condensed milk, thawed lemon- ade concentrate, and lemon peel; mix thoroughly. Fold in thawed whipped topping and pour into cooled crust. Chill several hours or overnight. Top with additional whipped topping and thin lemon slices.

❖ FUDGY BROWNIES   (Makes 2 dozen)

½ cup butter
 2 1-ounce squares unsweetened chocolate
 1 cup granulated sugar
 2 eggs
 1 teaspoon vanilla
¾ cup all-purpose flour

½ cup chopped walnuts
2½ cups sifted confectioners' sugar
¼ cup unsweetened cocoa
¼ cup butter, softened
 3 tablespoons boiling water
½ teaspoon vanilla extract

Preheat oven to 350° F. Grease an 8-by-8-by-2-inch square baking pan and set aside. In a saucepan, melt butter and chocolate over low heat, stirring constantly. Remove from heat and stir in the sugar, eggs, and vanilla, mixing well. Stir in flour and nuts. Spread batter into prepared pan and bake 30 minutes. Cool in pan on a wire rack. In a medium-size mixing bowl, combine confectioners' sugar, cocoa, butter, boiling water, and vanilla. Beat with electric mixer on low to medium speed until smooth. Cool until the frosting is of spreading consistency. Spread frosting on top of brownies. Cut into squares.

PEANUT BUTTER COOKIES (Makes 4 dozen)

½ cup creamy peanut butter
¼ cup shortening
¼ cup butter
1⅓ cups all-purpose flour
½ cup granulated sugar
½ cup brown sugar, packed

1 egg
1 teaspoon vanilla extract
½ teaspoon baking powder
½ teaspoon baking soda
   Granulated sugar

Preheat oven to 375° F. In a large mixing bowl, combine peanut butter, shortening, and butter; mix to combine. Add about half the flour, mixing well. Add ½ cup sugar, the brown sugar, egg, vanilla, baking powder, and baking soda. Beat until mixed well. Stir in remaining flour. Shape dough into 1-inch balls, roll balls in sugar, and place 2 inches apart on ungreased cookie sheet. Using the tines of a fork, form crisscross on top of each cookie, flattening dough to about ¼-inch thickness. Bake 9 to 11 minutes or just until the edges begin to brown. Remove from cookie sheet and cool on a wire rack.

CHERRY COBBLER WITH BISCUIT TOPPING (Serves 4)

¾ cup granulated sugar
1 tablespoon cornstarch
4 cups fresh pitted tart red cherries
3 tablespoons butter, divided
1 egg

1 tablespoon whole milk
½ cup all-purpose flour
1 tablespoon granulated sugar
¾ teaspoon baking powder
⅛ teaspoon salt

Preheat oven to 400° F. In a medium saucepan, combine ¾ cup sugar and cornstarch; mix well. Add cherries and ⅓ cup water. Cook over medium heat, stirring until slightly thickened. Stir in 1 tablespoon butter. Turn off heat. In a cup, mix egg and milk with a fork; set aside. In a medium bowl, combine flour, 1 tablespoon sugar, baking powder, and salt; mix well. Using a pastry blender, cut in 2 tablespoons butter until the mixture resembles coarse crumbs. Make a well in the center of the mixture and add egg mixture all at once. Stir with fork just until moistened. Pour hot cherry filling into an ungreased, 8-inch round baking dish. Spoon topping into 4 mounds on top and bake 20 to 25 minutes. Serve warm.

My Hometown

My hometown was a courthouse square,
The sound of friendly feet,
The store that sold red licorice
Just off the broad Main Street.

It was the weekly paper
That told every bit of news . . .
From what the preacher talked about
To sales of children's shoes.

It was an old man's meeting place,
A place to sit and chat.
It was the corner drugstore
And the sheriff's wide-brimmed hat.

It was the yearly county fair,
The 4-H girls and boys . . .
The sticky candy apples
And the dangling five-cent toys.

It was the single schoolhouse
And the bus that took us there . . .
The simple little gray stone church
For Sunday School and prayer.

My hometown in my childhood
Was a perfect place to be . . .
And when I long for happiness
I go back in memory.

Paula Zoe Burn

Cars of old line the sides of Main Street in Marlboro, Massachusetts.

*In 1936, choices were plentiful at
Whelan's Drugstore in New York City.*

*Memory is the diary we all
carry around with us.*

Oscar Wilde

AMERICAN GIRL

Mary Cantwell

*W*hen we marched up Hope Street on parade mornings, I with the end of the staff that flew the Girl Scout flag nestled next to my belly button, we were a sight. The Goldenrods and the Marigolds weren't in it with us. When we passed 232 Hope Street, stepping smartly, my family clapped and Gampa raised his hat—felt on Armistice Day, straw on Memorial—for the Stars and Stripes. When we stood near the flag-markered graves in North Burial Ground and the bugler played "Taps," I threw back my shoulders and presented a brave face to the west. And when, on the evening of Armistice Day, Ruthie and I walked along High Street after the service at the Train of Artillery Hall, through the rustling trees and the dry leaves and the damp air, after the speeches and "My Buddy" and "There's a Long, Long Trail a-Winding," we were too blissfully sorrowful to speak. How lovely it was to feel the tears flowing down your cheeks and know that no adult could tell you to stop that sniffling, because you were weeping in a good cause. . . .

Usually I grabbed every opportunity to put on my Girl Scout uniform and proclaim to the world my membership in a club, but not on the Fourth of July. Bristol's parade was the oldest in the country, and maybe the biggest, and I wouldn't have dreamed of marching in it. Miss the floats, the governor of Rhode Island, the drum-and-bugle corps from all over New England, the Fourth of July Committee with their ice-cream pants, boutonnières, and malacca canes, the antique cars and the fire engines and the servicemen from Newport and Jamestown and points north? Miss the balloon men and the eggnog Papa put in the punch bowl in the front hall and the thrill when some of the marchers—the governor, even—flourished their hats to his applause? . . .

> *Bristol's parade was the oldest in the country, and maybe the biggest.*

Drums are pounding in the distance, and cops on motorcycles are coming around the corner of Summer Street. Here they are: the Fourth of July Committee, swinging their canes and doffing their hats, the Colt Memorial High School Band . . . in their spanking green and white, Bristol's own bugle-and-drum corps, straight-backed, . . . bugles high and blasting.

In New Canaan, Connecticut, the annual Fourth of July parade was awaited by all.

Fife-and-drum corps in colonial outfits. Two men and a boy in tatters and bandages portraying the Spirit of '76. The *Quarante et Huit*, World War I veterans packed into a boxcar, plump and cheering. Shriners looking silly in their silks and fezzes. (One of the Barrington crowd is wearing his fez and three-fingers a conspiratorial salute.) Cesar B., Bristol's richest *Brava*, his brass-colored skin tarnished in the cold northern light, prancing on his palomino. Over all, the flag with the anchor that says "Hope" and the flag with the severed snake that says "Don't tread on me."

A wail, many wails, and the fire engines are bringing up the rear, with the boys of Bristol hanging from them like monkeys do from trees. Now Di and I can brush the grass off our shorts and hazard the bathrooms which, on Mother's order, have been the exclusive property of the Barrington crowd, not one of whom, she says, can hold it. Above us balloons have tangled themselves in the trees or drifted upward to push against the sky until they're out of sight, and their temporary custodians are sobbing into the lawn.

The afternoon is as flat as if someone has

The magical atmosphere of the fair is evident in artist A. Gwynne Jones's painting **A Fair at Night.**

candy, which sticks to our faces, and orange soda, which stains our mouths, and stands between our mounts on the merry-go-round. We are really too old for the merry-go-round, but he is not, and he is grinning as what he calls the dobby horses plunge up and down and the Common spins around us.

The games are shaded by a square of canvas tethered to four poles and we stand in the umber light with the rest of Bristol's gamblers, tossing pennies into numbered squares and rings around milk bottles. Next we try to fool the man who guesses weights by puffing our cheeks, and get our fortunes told by a battered automaton in a windowed box. A tall dark man is in my future. . . .

The Ferris wheel is the centerpiece of the carnival, and we save it for last, settling into the gently swaying seats with a sigh. Our feet are sore and our eyes runny and we have breathed too long of dust and cotton candy and motor oil. Up here, though, up here on the top of the Ferris wheel, our faces are brushed by the salt-laced wind that is fingering the tops of the elms. With Gampa, whose arms enclose us, we survey our domain. Bristol lies before us, as neat and tidy as it would appear on an aerial map.

If we look to the left we can see the grease-pole contest and the water fight between the fire battalions and, behind them, lowering

put a lid on it. Papa and Mother are at the chief marshall's reception; Esther is off somewhere with one of the girls from the shop; Ganny is in her rocker, scouring the *Providence Journal;* and Gampa is on the Connerys' back steps talking to Old Man Connery. There is nothing for Di and me to do but sit in the playroom, packing and unpacking the trunks of our Dy-Dee dolls, reading our Judy Morton books, and coloring our entries to the Dixie Dugan dress-design contest. Until Gampa decides, that is, that the air has cooled and the sun is low enough for us to go up to the Common and the carnival.

Summer's heat has settled on the Common and the yellow dust rises up to meet it, sifting through our sandals and our socks and lodging between our toes. Gampa buys us cotton over Wood Street, St. Mary's Church, its rectory, and the convent for the parochial school nuns. Down on the corner is the old town cemetery, its worn gravestones half-swallowed by tall, coarse grass. "How many people are dead in there?" Papa likes to sing out as we walk toward church on Sunday. "All of them!" we chorus.

We can see the bandstand in the center of the Common, and the men setting up the folding chairs for the concert to be given by the Portuguese Independent Band. Our Lady of Mount Carmel, the Italian church, is to the right, and beyond it we can see the spires of St Elizabeth's, the Portuguese church.

The Walley School is straight ahead, windows closed, shades drawn, silent as a clam. A strip of grass separates it from the Baptist church, and a broader strip runs between the church and the old courthouse. At the corner the Byfield School stares at the Reynolds School across the street, each of them as shuttered and as secret as the Walley. If we could peer through the trees that fringe the Common—but no, the leaves are too thick in summer—we could see Bristol Harbor, and sailboats on their last tack.

The sun is setting, and the men of the Portuguese Independent Band have taken their seats in the bandstand. A drum roll, and "Lady of Spain" crashes through the still, hot air. Fireworks star the sky and Roman candles shoot up from the backyards on Wood Street.

It's time to walk home, past porches from which we can hear low voices and the squeak of gliders. . . . Soon we'll be on our own

porch, spooning up coffee ice cream from Buffington's and listening to the boom of fireworks from over Poppasquash way.

With the sun gone, the air is damp as a used towel, and the scent of low tide is drifting up from the foot of Union Street. The cars have all gone back to Providence and Taunton and maybe even as far as Boston, and the cleaning trucks have already swept through town. Di and I are perched on the porch railing, and Ganny and Gampa are settled in their wicker chairs; and the coffee ice cream is puddling in Ganny's little glass bowls. "Isn't this a nice party?" Gampa says, happy because he wants no more at this moment than this wife, these grandchildren, and this house.

The Ferris Wheel was always the top attraction at the carnival.

THE BANDSTAND IN THE PARK

Donna Lebrecht

Remember those days when pastimes were simple and leisure summer afternoons were whiled away at concerts in the park?

There was the soft sighing sound of the wind in the trees that mingled gently with the sounds of the people as they gathered. First the band members would arrive, setting up amid the metallic clink of instruments, softly spoken words and the scuffling of their feet against the old wood floor of the bandstand. Quiet, busy sounds.

And then, right on their heels, the sounds of the children of the town streaming into the park with exuberant shouts and whistles as they ran on ahead of their folks, calling out each other's names and darting into leafy bowers for games of hide-and-seek.

Now, coming more quietly behind, the voices of the townsfolk themselves were heard as they gathered slowly before the bandstand, saying hello and exchanging bits of gossip with neighbors and friends while their eyes searched out their children in the crowd.

Melody after melody rolled through those summer afternoons.

Dressed in their Sunday best, they slowly settled upon the green wooden benches lined up before the preparing band.

"Tap, tap." The bandleader rapped them to attention. And then with a smile and a jaunty bow he turned quickly on his heel, gave a magnificent sweep with his baton, and the quiet afternoon suddenly exploded with the sound of one of Sousa's marches!

How that music rang out on the sweet summer air, rolling out across the green, bounding to the treetops, and filling all the sky! Instantly a hundred hearts became as one. Feet tapped, faces smiled, and shoulders swayed as the people were caught up in the rhythm and the beauty of that music in the park.

Meanwhile the children played and shouted and raced noisily about. There was the loud, long squeal of protest from the old hand pump whenever someone sought a drink, and here and there a squirrel scolded from the treetops;

In 1905, the park was perfect for not only concerts, but a little sailing as well.

but they were just noises in the background, to be sure. For, as if not hearing them at all, the band played gaily on, not missing a single beat. Melody after melody rolled through those summer afternoons and every heart and soul found happiness in the music of each tune.

On and on it went, the march and then a polka and then a march again, interspersed with roars of applause that burst forth at the end of each song. How sweet was that summer afternoon as overhead the sun curved slowly across the sky, shadows began to lengthen, and then the day began to die.

Yet the music lingered on and, softened by the shadows, the marches gradually gave way to the romantic little melodies popular in that day. The wind grew just a bit more chill and

the sky a bit more blue; and sweethearts, sitting closer now, sometimes sneaked a kiss or two. Grandma patted Grandpa's knee and smiled up at him and Dad even put his arm around Mom, her waist still girlishly slim.

A hundred little romances went with the music as it grew dark and a hundred happy people were gathered round that bandstand in the park.

Memory is the golden bridge
That keeps our hearts in touch
With all the long-past yesterdays
And things we loved so much.

Georgia B. Adams

The Circus-Day Parade

Oh, the circus-day parade!
How the bugles played and played!
And how the glossy horses tossed
their flossy manes and neighed,
As the rattle and the rhyme
of the tenor-drummer's time
Filled all the hungry hearts of us
with melody sublime!

How the grand bandwagon shone
with a splendor all its own,
And glittered with a glory
that our dreams had never known!
And how the boys behind,
high and low of every kind,
Marched in unconscious capture,
with a rapture undefined!

How the horsemen, two and two,
with their plumes of white and blue,
And crimson, gold and purple,
nodding by at me and you,
Waved the banners that they bore,
as the knights in days of yore,
Till our glad eyes gleamed
and glistened like the spangles that they wore!

How the graceless-graceful stride
of the elephant was eyed,
And the capers of the little horse
that cantered at his side!
How the shambling camels, tame
to the plaudits of their fame,
With listless eyes came silent;
masticating as they came.

How the cages jolted past,
with each wagon battened fast,
And the mystery within it only hinted of at last
From the little grated square
in the rear, and nosing there
The snout of some strange animal
that sniffed the outer air!

And, last of all, the clown,
making mirth for all the town,
With his lips curved ever upward
And his eyebrows ever down,
And his chief attention paid
to the little mule that played
A tattoo on the dashboard
with his heels, in the parade.

Oh! the circus-day parade!
How the bugles played and played!
And how the glossy horses tossed
their flossy manes and neighed,
As the rattle and the rhyme
of the tenor-drummer's time
Filled all the hungry hearts of us
with melody sublime!

The elephant march announces the arrival of the circus.

James Whitcomb Riley

Small moments lie as jewels on the velvet of memory, sparkling into newness at a thought, wrapped untarnished in the kind and mystic veils of time, to glow again, the brighter for the remembering.

Glen Pritchard

Every child watched in awe as the lion tamer performed.

The elaborate, gilded band wagon was not to be missed in this circus parade.

HOMETOWN ENTERTAINMENT

Hometowns of the past offered few amusements as tempting as a new movie playing at the theater or the news that the circus parade was on its way. Even the most casual requests of parents were fulfilled readily as every child did his best to earn the reward of a day of entertainment by dancing elephants under the big top or Hollywood stars in the latest feature film. For days after the excitement, favorite performances and acrobatic feats were enthusiastically re-created in the backyards of small-town America.

The first motion-picture production company to use synchronized sound in a silent film was founded by four American brothers: the Warner brothers.

The Warner brothers opened a nickelodeon (an early movie theater named for its nickel admission price) in New Castle, Pennsylvania, in 1903.

As the film industry moved gradually to Hollywood, independent producers such as Cecil B. De Mille and Mack Sennett set up their own studios and introduced America to slapstick with such comics as Charlie Chaplin. The golden age of silent film had begun.

Screen comedy made its mark in the 1920s with two comedians, Harold Lloyd and Buster Keaton, joining the legendary Charlie Chaplin in the forefront.

In 1927, Warner Brothers released *The Jazz Singer*, its first "talking picture."

Colorful circus posters on the sides of barns and fences were a welcome reminder of coming attractions and became part of the American landscape.

Rather than trying to manage the limited roads available during the late nineteenth century, circuses soon turned to trains and quickly traveled from one performance to another. In the 1890s, riding the rails took the Barnum and Bailey Circus eighty-five cars, enough to carry more than one thousand circus employees, five rings and stages, and the largest traveling menagerie in the world.

First introduced in America in 1792, circuses were dominated by equestrian shows; but the first few decades introduced juggling, acrobatic acts, wild-animal acts, and clowns. It wasn't until 1859 that audiences would thrill to early flying trapeze acts.

The big top, or tent, which enclosed the circus festivities was often set up in a pasture or field near the edge of town.

In 1889, the Ringling Brothers Circus had a seating capacity of four thousand and charged a fifty-cent admission for adults and one quarter for children.

STREETLIGHTS

Marion McGuire

When I was nine, the only streetlight in Strawberry Park was at the corner of Normandie and Amestory—a single, dim, bug-covered bulb suspended by four long wires that cast a faint golden puddle on the asphalt roads. My mother, just learning to drive her 1926 Dodge, always stopped there at night and peered in all directions. She said that corners attracted traffic. "You may not see a car for miles," she said, "but just get to the intersection, and there will be another driver."

Although I was unsympathetic to her driving troubles, always giggling when she came to a hill and had to back down again because she had forgotten to shift, I truly wanted her to succeed. Without a car I would never see a movie. Strawberry Park had no theater; the nearest movie house was in Hollywood, twelve miles away. Searchlights from premiere showings sometimes swept across our dark valley like diamond highways to heaven, but the glittering world of show business remained out of my reach.

Sometimes I read the movie ads in *The Los Angeles Times* in an effort to coax my mother to drive into town. "Listen," I would say. "How about *Love Makes 'Em Wild* or *Slaves of Beauty*?"

"Oh, such suggestive

> *Searchlights from premiere showings sometimes swept across our valley like diamond highways.*

titles!" exclaimed Mother, who frowned on many earthly pleasures. And there was another obstacle: the PTA list of films recommended for children. Neither *Love Makes 'Em Wild* nor *Slaves of Beauty* made the list. So I was left movieless, to whine and sulk and dream of bright lights somewhere down the road of life.

Then, in August of 1928, the *Times* announced a new theater, coming soon, at the corner of Manchester and Vermont streets, five miles from Strawberry Park. The new theater was named The Fox, and the advertisement was seductive—weekend double bills, low prices (ten cents for children), a noon box-office opening, five acts of vaudeville. I couldn't wait to go.

After checking the PTA list, Mother was not enthusiastic. None of the movies were approved. Her driving, however, had greatly improved, and only one small hill rose between our house and The Fox. "I'll tell you this Marion,"

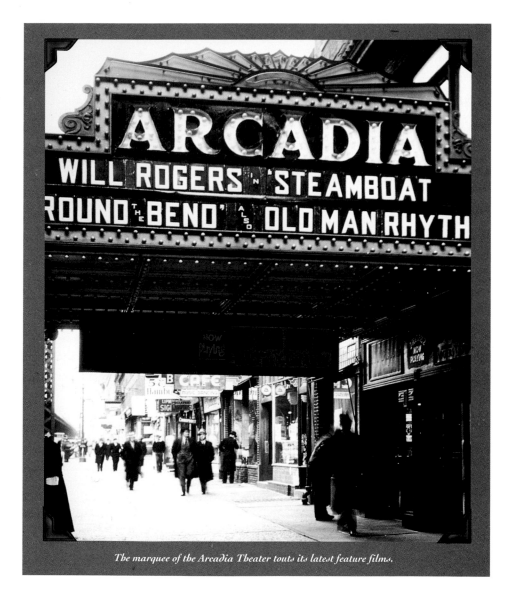

The marquee of the Arcadia Theater touts its latest feature films.

she said. "When and if there is a movie up there for children, I will take you."

On the strength of this announcement, I saved my nickels for the next two weeks, just in case. One Sunday after church Mother decided to drive north on Vermont just for fun. . . . She rolled smoothly over little Athens Hill and did not have to stop until she

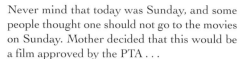

Moviegoers brave the weather to enjoy a performance at the Paramount Theater in New York City.

came to the corner of Vermont and Manchester. There, directly in front of us, was The Fox—three stories of yellow stucco topped with two ceramic torches spouting fake flames. The film on the marquee was *With Admiral Byrd at the South Pole*.

Now Mother was a hero worshipper, and Admiral Byrd was way up on her list beside Charles Lindbergh and Teddy Roosevelt.

Never mind that today was Sunday, and some people thought one should not go to the movies on Sunday. Mother decided that this would be a film approved by the PTA . . .

It was a very white movie, full of swirling snow, and Mother was spellbound. Certainly neither of us was aware of what awaited us outside.

When we emerged from the theater, a dense, white fog had rolled in, not unlike the clouds at the South Pole. Mother could not see the road and had to drive with her head out the window, guided by the black seams in the road. Once she drove into someone's strawberry field and felt lucky to ever get out again. When we finally turned into our own driveway, she sighed wearily and said, "Well, honey, we won't try that again, will we?" I was sure my movie days were over forever.

Several years passed, and movies went on without us. I was almost too old to get in for a dime when one day The Fox advertised *The Little Minister* with Katherine Hepburn. The PTA approved, Mother approved (Saturday only), and she agreed to drive me up when the box office opened at noon. . . . She would come back for me at five o'clock, before dark.

We reached the theater exactly at noon, and a line had already formed at the box office. I was afraid that all the seats would be sold before I got in, so I paid scant attention to Mother's final admonition, "Five o'clock. Don't make me wait." I rushed in a panic to the line, but my worry was unfounded. The theater was half empty. I followed the usherette down the carpeted aisle and sank gratefully into a plush seat.

The house darkened, and a screen appeared. I watched the Pathe News, a cartoon, a Hoot Gibson western, an episode in a weekly serial, and several previews for coming attractions. Then the lights came on again, the mighty Wurlitzer organ roared, and hundreds of tiny Meglan Kiddies came on stage tap dancing. Five acts of vaudeville followed, as advertised, and I was completely enchanted.

The lights came on again; the mighty Wurlitzer organ roared.

When the final dancers clicked their way into the wings, I glanced up at the clock high up on the wall beside the stage curtain. The hour hand was pointing to five.

I rushed up the aisle, past the box office to the curb, and there was the Dodge with Mother opening the door for me. I howled, "But I haven't seen it yet. It didn't come on."

Mother got out of the car and stepped up to the girl in the box office. "I thought you were showing *The Little Minister*," she said.

"Not until five fifteen," said the girl. "It's the beginning of our evening show."

"My little girl still has her ticket," said Mother, checking the soggy paper in my wet palm. "Can she go back in?"

The girl nodded.

Mother said, "All right, honey. I'll be back when it's over." She gave me a pat and sent me through the door.

Whatever adventures Katherine Hepburn had in *The Little Minister* escaped me. My mind was outside, thinking of my mother driving slowly along dark, foggy streets, making wrong turns, grinding gears, weeping, and all because of a selfish, greedy daughter.

The picture ended, and I ran outside to the car waiting at the curb. Mother started the engine and opened the door. I jumped in. We did not speak. She shifted into reverse, signalled, shifted into low, pulled into the traffic, and then headed toward Athens Hill.

"Just wait till we get to the top, Marion," she said. "You won't believe the sight."

When we reached the top, I looked down into our usually dark valley, and I saw a beautiful shining necklace of diamond streetlights outlining Vermont Avenue as far as I could see.

"See," said Mother, "if you wait long enough, everything works out." And we coasted happily down the hill.

Gentle Twilight

The gentle twilight wraps a soft blue shawl
About the shoulders of the drowsy day
And pins it with a single star. The call
Of mothers brings the children in from play
To prayers, and bed. Beyond the mountain's rim
The blacksmith, night, is forging a new moon
Into a shining cutlass; and the hymn
The katydids and crickets softly croon
Hangs in the quiet air.
God must look down, and smile,
Upon the peace of this small town.

Jessie Wilmore Murton

A Fence, a Farm, and a Family Cow:
MEMORIES OF THE COUNTRY

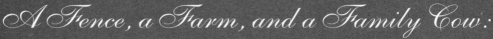

A Country Road

I'm searching for a country road
Embraced by an old rail fence
That frames a flowered meadow
Or a lovely woodland dense.

Where the elm and the oak and the maple
Lift leafy arms to pray,
And the oriole and the robin
Rejoice in the warmth of the day.

I'm searching for a country road
Where the heart can soar and sing,
Where the sun pours down its golden wealth
And soft winds lightly cling.

Where new leaves rustle a muted song,
The sky is freshly blue,
And the flocks and herds in the meadow
Ask, "Mere mortal, who are you?"

I'm searching for a country road
Where a traveler, passing by,
May find brown pebbles to scuff along
Or toss toward cloudless skies.

Where can I find this lonely road
So rustic and carefree?
It once served a past generation
And fills my memories.

Lucille Crumley

*Farmers near the end of a long day in Henry H. Parker's
painting* **A Surrey Cornfield Near Reigate.**

THE BOHEMIAN GIRL

Willa Cather

O n the day of Olaf Ericson's barn-raising, his wife, for once in a way, rose early. Johanna Vavrika had been baking cakes and frying and boiling and spicing meats for a week beforehand, but it was not until the day before the party was to take place that Clara showed any interest in it. Then she was seized with one of her fitful spasms of energy, and took the wagon and little Eric and spent the day on Plum Creek, gathering vines and swamp goldenrod to decorate the barn.

By four o'clock in the afternoon buggies and wagons began to arrive at the big unpainted building in front of Olaf's house. When Nils and his mother came at five, there were more than fifty people in the barn, and a great drove of children. On the ground floor stood six long tables, set with the crockery of seven flourishing Ericson families, lent for the occasion. . . . In one corner of the barn, behind a pile of green-and-white-striped watermelons, was a circle of chairs for the old people; the younger guests sat on bushel measures or barbed-wire spools, and the children tumbled about in the haymow. The box stalls Clara had converted into booths. The framework was hidden by goldenrod and sheaves of wheat, and the partitions were covered with wild grapevines full of fruit. At one of these Johanna Vavrika watched over her cooked meats, enough to provision an army; and at the next her kitchen girls had arranged the ice-cream freezers, and Clara was already cutting pies and cakes against the hour of serving. At the third stall, little Hilda, in a bright pink lawn dress, dispensed lemonade throughout the afternoon. Olaf, as a public man, had thought it inadvisable to serve beer in his barn. . . .

The sun, pouring in at the big doors, filled the whole interior with a golden light.

"Hasn't Cousin Clara fixed things lovely?" little Hilda whispered, when Nils went up to her stall and asked for lemonade.

Nils leaned against the booth, talking to the excited little girl and watching the people. The barn faced the west, and the sun, pouring in at the big doors, filled the whole interior with a golden light, through which filtered fine particles of dust from the haymow, where the children were romping. . . . The older women, having assured themselves that there were twenty kinds of cake, not

At an old-fashioned barn raising, working together makes a difficult task enjoyable.

47

counting cookies, and three dozen fat pies, repaired to the corner behind the pile of watermelons, put on their white aprons, and fell to

They were a fine company of old women, and a Dutch painter would have loved to find them there together.

their knitting and fancywork. They were a fine company of old women, and a Dutch painter would have loved to find them there together, where the sun made bright patches on the floor and sent long, quivering shafts of gold through the dusky shade up among the rafters. There

were fat, rosy old women who looked hot in their best black dresses; spare, alert old women with brown, dark-veined hands; and several of almost heroic frame, not less massive than old Mrs. Ericson herself. Few of them wore glasses, and old Mrs. Svendsen, a Danish woman, who was quite bald, wore the only cap among them. Mrs. Oleson, who had twelve big grandchildren, could still show two braids of yellow hair as thick as her own wrists. Among all these grandmothers there were more brown heads than white. They all had a pleased, prosperous air, as if they were more than satisfied with themselves and with life. Nils, leaning against Hilda's lemonade stand, watched them as they sat chattering in four languages, their fingers never lagging behind their tongues.

"Look at them over there," he whispered, detaining Clara as she passed him. "Aren't they the Old Guard? I've just counted thirty hands. I guess they've wrung many a chicken's neck and warmed many a boy's jacket for him in their time."

In reality he fell into amazement when he thought of the Herculean labors those fifteen pairs of hands had performed: of the cows they had milked, the butter they had made, the gardens they had planted, the chil-

Two young girls ride by their barn-raising brigade on their way to help with refreshments.

dren and grandchildren they had tended, the brooms they had worn out, the mountains of food they had cooked. It made him dizzy.

The barn supper began at six o'clock and lasted for two hilarious hours. . . . While the supper was being cleared away the two fiddlers began to tune up for the dance. Clara was to accompany them on her old upright piano, which had been brought down from her father's. By this time Nils had renewed old acquaintances. Since his interview with Clara in the cellar, he had been busy telling all the old women how young they looked, and all the young ones how pretty they

A cool slice of watermelon at the barn supper offers welcome relief after a hard day.

were, and assuring the men that they had here the best farmland in the world. He had made himself so agreeable that old Mrs. Ericson's friends began to come up to her and tell how lucky she was to get her smart son back again, and please to get him to play his flute. Joe Vavrika, who could still play very well when he forgot that he had rheumatism, caught up a fiddle from Johnny Oleson and played a crazy Bohemian dance tune that set the wheels going. When he dropped the bow every one was ready to dance.

Olaf, in a frock coat and a solemn made-up necktie, led the grand march with his mother. . . .

The musicians grinned, looked at each other, hesitated, and began a new air; and Nils sang with them, as the couples fell from a quick waltz to a long, slow glide:

"When other lips and other hearts
    Their tale of love shall tell,
In language whose excess imparts
    The power they feel so well."

The old cowmen applauded vigorously. "What a gay one he is, that Nils!" And old Mrs. Svendsen's cap lurched dreamily from side to side to the flowing measure of the dance.

"Of days that have as ha-a-p-py been,
    And you'll remember me."

Down in the Valley

1. Down in the val - ley, the val - ley so low, Hang your head
2. Writ - ing this let - ter, con-tain-ing three lines, An - swer my
3. Ros - es love sun - shine, vi - o - lets love dew, An - gels in

o - ver, hear the wind blow. Hear the wind
ques - tion, will you be mine? Will you be
heav - en, know I love you. Know I love

blow, dear, hear the wind blow, Hang your head
mine, dear, will you be mine? An - swer my
you, dear, know I love you, An - gels in

o - ver, hear the wind blow.
ques - tion, will you be mine?
heav - en, know I love you.

A family farm can be seen from this rural dirt road in Reading, Vermont.

A RIBBON FOR BALDY

Jesse Stuart

*A*s I grow older, I constantly rediscover the beauty of the land where I was born and where I still live today. This valley becomes more valuable and precious to me every day. It has been and still is the source of my work as a writer.

One day as I walked over my land, I remembered that I wasn't the only writer who had explored and used his own backyard for inspiration. Emily Dickinson, Henry David Thoreau, Nathaniel Hawthorne, and Robert Frost are just four who have done so. And so I was grateful to the land for what it had given me as a human being and as a writer.

On another day, as I stood by the W-Hollow stream listening to its sound, I thought of Old Baldy. Old Baldy is one of three cone-shaped hills that you can see if you stand on the ridge overlooking the valley. These three hills are independent of the other hills that enclose the valley; they are separate formations and very unusual.

The highest of these hills looked like a giant wigwam. It was part of the first fifty acres my father ever bought. Since much of his farm was pastureland, we needed to use as much land as we could for farming. We had to grow feed for our domestic animals and corn and wheat for our meal and flour. So we had to use the cone-shaped hill. We called it Old Baldy. We cleared Old Baldy from bottom to top. Then I plowed it, breaking the roots with a bulltongue plow. I drove my team of mules around and around the hill like a corkscrew until I reached the top. Then when I laid off a furrow in which to plant the corn, I began at the bottom and went around and around again all the way to the top, making one long row of corn. It was the longest row of corn in this valley, the longest row in eastern Kentucky, and maybe in the whole country.

When we were asked by our teacher in general science in Greenup High School to write about the most unusual thing we had ever done or seen, I wrote about this row of corn. And I had the most unusual paper in my class. This was one of my themes that I never kept. And now, I went back to this cone-shaped hill which we used to call Baldy and memories of high school days came back to me. Now Baldy and I had time to renew our friendship; I thought about this paper I had written. And one day I sat on a mossy stone under a poplar tree near the base of Baldy and rewrote that theme. Later, my wife Naomi gave it the title of "A Ribbon for Baldy," and I sent it to a magazine where it was accepted as a story. This factual article, which became a story, was written in a day. It was written of experiences I had lived in my association with this piece of earth while I was a student in Greenup High.

I was grateful to the land for what it had given me.

The day Professor Herbert started talking about a project for each member of our General Science class, I was more excited than I had ever been. I wanted to have an outstanding project. I wanted it to be greater, to be more unusual than those of my classmates. I wanted to do something worthwhile, and something to make them respect me.

I'd made the best grade in my class in General Science. I'd made more yardage, more tackles and carried the football across the goal line more times than any player on my team. But making good grades and playing rugged football hadn't made them forget that I rode a mule to school, that I had worn my mother's shoes the first

year and that I slipped away at the noon hour so no one would see me eat fat pork between slices of corn bread.

Every day I thought about my project for the General Science class. We had to have our project by the end of the school year and it was now January.

In the classroom, in study hall and when I did odd jobs on my father's fifty acres, I thought about my project. But it wouldn't come to me like an algebra problem or memorizing a poem. I couldn't think of a project that would help my father and mother to support us. One that would be good and useful.

"If you set your mind on something and keep on thinking about it, the idea will eventually come," Professor Herbert told us when

Men, machines, and animals work alongside each other to prepare a field for spring planting.

The farmer can admire his field from the nearby farmhouse.

Bascom Wythe complained about how hard it was to find a project.

One morning in February I left home in a white cloud that had settled over the deep valleys. I could not see an object ten feet in front of me in this mist. I crossed the pasture into the orchard and the mist began to thin. When I reached the ridge road, the light, thin air was clear of mist. I looked over the sea of rolling white clouds. The tops of the dark winter hills jutted up like little islands.

I have to ride a mule, but not one of my classmates lives in a prettier place, I thought, as I surveyed my world. Look at Little Baldy! What a pretty island in the sea of clouds. A thin ribbon of cloud seemed to envelop cone-shaped Little Baldy from bottom to top like the new rope Pa had just bought for the windlass over our well.

Then, like a flash—the idea for my project came to me. And what an idea it was! I'd not tell anybody about it! I wouldn't even tell my father, but I

knew he'd be for it. Little Baldy wrapped in the white coils of mist had given me the idea for it.

I was so happy I didn't care who laughed at me, what anyone said or who watched me eat fat meat on corn bread for my lunch. I had an idea and I knew it was a wonderful one.

"I've got something to talk over with you," I told Pa when I got home. "Look over there at that broom-sedge and the scattered pines on Little Baldy. I'd like to burn the broom-sedge and briers and cut the pines and farm that this summer."

We stood in our barnlot and looked at Little Baldy.

"Yes, I've been thinkin' about clearin' that hill up someday," Pa said.

"Pa, I'll clear up all this south side and you clear up the other side," I said. "And I'll plow all of it and we'll get it in corn this year."

"Now this will be some undertakin'," he said. "I can't clear that land up and work six days a week on the railroad section. But if you

A farmer and his one-horse corn planter make their way through the field.

will clear up the south side, I'll hire Bob Lavender to do the other side."

"That's a bargain," I said.

That night while the wind was still and the broom-sedge and leaves were dry, my father and I set fire all the way around the base. Next morning Little Baldy was a dark hill jutting high into February's cold, windy sky.

Pa hired Bob Lavender to clear one portion and I started working on the other. I worked early of mornings before I went to school. I hurried home and worked into the night.

Finn, my ten-year-old brother, was big enough to help me saw down the scattered pines with a crosscut. With a hand-spike I started the logs rolling and they rolled to the base of Little Baldy.

By middle March, I had my side cleared. Bob Lavender had finished his too. We burned the brush and I was ready to start plowing.

By April 15th I had plowed all of Little Baldy. My grades in school had fallen off some. Bascom Wythe made the highest mark in General Science and he had always wanted to pass me in this subject. But I let him make the grades.

If my father had known what I was up to, he might not have let me do it. But he was going early to work on the railway section and he never got home until nearly dark. So when I laid Little Baldy off to plant him in corn, I started at the bottom and went around and around this high cone-shaped hill like a corkscrew. I was three days reaching the top. Then, with a hand planter, I planted the corn on moonlit nights.

When I showed my father what I'd done, he looked strangely at me. Then he said, "What made you do a thing like this? What's behind all of this?"

"I'm going to have the longest corn row in the world," I said. "How long do you think it is, Pa?"

"That row is over twenty miles," Pa said, laughing.

Finn and I measured the corn row with a rod pole and it was 23.5 miles long.

When it came time to report on our projects and I stood up in class and said I had a row of corn on our hill farm 23.5 miles long, everybody laughed. But when I told how I got the idea and how I had worked to accomplish my project, everybody was silent.

Professor Herbert and the General Science class hiked to my home on a Saturday in early May when the young corn was pretty and green in the long row. Two newspapermen from a neighboring town came too, and a photographer took pictures of Little Baldy and his ribbon of corn. He took pictures of me, of my home and parents and also of Professor Herbert and my classmates.

When the article and pictures were published, a few of my classmates got a little jealous of me but not one of them ever laughed at me again. And my father and mother were the proudest two parents any son could ever hope to have.

THE LANE

Janice Porter Hayes

*I*f gratitude is a virtue, I learned it walking the country lane of our family farm.

As a child, the lane seemed long and rutty, its dusty kisses covering our feet. Chinese Elms marched down one side of the lane, Father's haystack following the other. The lane led to the outside world; to the waiting school bus, the brimming mailbox, and to the oil road leading into town. Down that country lane, I discovered nature, the universe, and the hand of God—especially on summer evenings after the sun had disappeared.

"Let's take a walk."

That was Father's signal for whomever wanted to follow. Together, we stepped into the cooling night, breath drawn as a full moon lit the sky. Slowly, we moved through the front yard and down the lane. Gravel crunched, and the day's dust settled around us. If luck was ours, a gentle breeze stirred the elms' leaves and we heard cows in the distance.

None of us spoke. Not until Father looked into the sky and said, "Stars look bright tonight. Sure is pretty."

Silence broken, we'd jostle and point, each trying to find the Big Dipper first. Then Orion. Then the North Star. If there were clouds, we'd watch them chase the moon, or swallow it whole. We'd find Venus, Mars or Jupiter. Sometimes, we smelled rain in the air.

Upon reaching the end of the lane, we'd stop; though sometimes, we'd walk out onto the oil road just enough to let the asphalt warm our feet. Then Father would look up into the elm trees.

"I remember how small the trees were when we moved to this farm years ago. Look at them now. Some people call them trash trees, but not me. I love them.

> *Down that country lane, I discovered nature, the universe, and the hand of God.*

Look how big the trees near the ditch are. They enjoy lots of water there."

We nodded, listening to the leaves whisper, Father's head cocked as if understanding them. Then he'd sigh, and say, "Me and your mother think this place is heaven." And so it was. Heaven, earth, tree, dust, hay, and water—all together in a single place.

C. S. Lewis once said that gratitude exclaims, quite properly, "How good of God to give me this." And so I felt about our country lane, even later when I'd wake early to milk the family cow or throw hay to our sleepy-eyed horses. Seeing life as my father saw it while strolling down our country lane, I'd notice the warm smell of an animal's hide, or the way its breath played like clouds in the frosty morning chill.

Even now, watching the trees in my own backyard, or following the play of sunlight on distant mountain peaks, I can't help but think, "How very good of God to give me this. How good of Him to share the moon and stars and clouds and trees; life and family with me. How very good of Him. How very, very good."

I consider it the best part of an education to have been born and brought up in the country. . . . There is virtue in country houses, in gardens and orchards, in fields, streams, and groves, in rustic recreations and plain manners, that neither cities nor universities enjoy.

Amos Bronson Alcott

A peaceful country lane connects rural farms and families.

THE FAMILY COW

R. J. McGinnis

The family cow, as she was known down through the years, was a symbol of family life, the hub around which the little world of the small town and the farm revolved. Those of us who cared for her, and subjected ourselves to the iron discipline of milking and feeding her and bedding her twice a day, 365 days a year, know that we got something from her besides the milk and butter curds.

We undoubtedly have a better milk supply since the family cow's demise, and we have a sounder and more efficient dairy economy. But there was something about the family cow that made up for her lack of high production.

When Bossy went, she went quickly. I milked a family cow and I'm not an old man, but it appears I may well have milked a family cow about as recently as any family cow milker, because between the time I sold my herd and went away to school and the day I returned from World War II, the family cow faded away.

When my family moved to a small town south of Des Moines in the early thirties, our family cow provided a family of five with all the milk we could drink, and we drank a great deal. We had a little benchtype separator and Mother made cottage cheese and reamed it and we ate this by the ton, mixed with grape jelly.

From the cream we made butter, and we used plenty of that. Father had all the buttermilk he wanted, and he loved the stuff. When my herd was at full strength—three milkers, three resters and a calf, I sold raw milk in gallon buckets on a nice little route. I delivered every day on a bicycle, hanging the little covered buckets on my handlebars. It was legal; it was profitable; and some of the time it was fun.

But Bossy's contribution in dollars and cents is not what I miss, although she made a very real contribution, at two bits a gallon, to my high school and college expenses. It is the friendship of the cows themselves, the management practices (some strange, indeed) through which farm animals were adapted to small-town living, and the way in which daily chores contributed to the growing up of boys that come to my mind when I think of Molly, Polly, and Sue.

All of our cows were characters. I've talked to other ex-family cow people and all of their cows were characters too.

We probably had a dozen cows from the time we bought Molly for eighteen dollars at a community sale until I sold the noble Frieda to pay my first year's college tuition. Yet, I can remember every cow by name, what we fed to each one, how much milk they gave, how many calves they had and when, and the sex of each of these and their names. Everything around our place had a name, even the turtle that lived in a hole under the kitchen.

I can remember winging home from school after Mother called the principal to report that Susie had broken down the fence around our little lot and eaten Mrs. McClellan's grapes. Not just once—often. That was why we finally sold her at the community sale.

Then we got Dolly. Dolly calved a month early and I found her bull calf lying in the cold mud. He was worth $1.50 for veal and nothing whatsoever for any other purpose. Still, it was a victory when he revived under the stove in the kitchen.

But Molly, perhaps because she was my first venture, was always my first love, in spite of her wanderings. She was a rangy beast, covered all over with red hair, and she had a great voice, clarion-clear, full-throated, with fine tone and character. She bellowed at the slightest provocation.

I thought the world of Molly but Father thought differently. We traded her for a smaller,

more settled type, with less voice and greater power of production.

Our next animal was Polly. Like Molly, she broke out all the time. We sold her for beef and got Frieda.

Frieda's acquisition marked a new peak in our cow business. All through the Susie-Polly-Molly era, we'd dreamed of some day having a really good cow. Near town was

A dairy farmer feeds his Holsteins.

a dairyman with an excellent herd. We'd visited there often. He announced a dispersal of his herd and I wasted no time in getting out to his place. Frieda was a standout—four-year-old, well built, of good mixed blood, and fresh.

The dairyman wouldn't sell her ahead of the sale—she'd been advertised and he said it wouldn't be honest. But he did do one thing — he promised me he'd sell her first, and at that kind of sale big buyers frequently didn't get warmed up until well after the sale had started.

This farmgirl's favorite chore is feeding her prize Guernsey calf.

I had $85 in the bank and drew a cashier's check for all of it. When the bidding opened I started boldly.

Bidding went to $80 all too quickly. This was to have been my limit, for trucking her home would cost $4 and I wanted some lunch. But we soon passed the $80 mark — in 50-cent and finally 25-cent bids — and I kept going. Unbelievably she was struck off to me at $84.25. We walked home — four miles in the dark with rebellious Frieda on the end of a rope.

Roughage, not grain, was the biggest feed-ing problem in the handling of a town cow. Each fall I cut sweet corn fodder from every garden in our end of town and carted it home on a wagon. You can get a whole shock of sweet corn fodder on a wagon if you tie it on right.

Saturdays I worked all day for a load of hay. It mattered little how much a day's work was worth or what hay was bring-ing — you pitched hay for a farmer and then brought the last load home. I'd take the horses back on Sunday morning.

To house the cow, I spent hours insulating the old carriage shed with cardboard cartons and rigging plumbing from old gut-ters. This contraption led from the pump near the house to the barnyard, where it emptied into a sawed-off barrel.

You hear tales about milking in the dark by the light of an old kerosene lantern, morning and night every day all winter, and milking outdoors morning and night all sum-mer. I did all those things.

For pasture, we either staked out the cows in the wide ditches along the highway or rented pasture from elderly ladies who lived on the edge of town.

There were two lovely ladies — one a widow and the other a spinster — who had pas-ture for rent. They, too, had cows. Cows are gregarious and thrive on company. Town cows get lonely. They wear themselves out bawling and patrolling the fence, leaning methodically on every post, and making very little milk.

I used to walk to pasture and milk there rather than drive the cows back and forth. Feed was served in a dishpan. It was up to the milker to finish milking before the cow finished eating and walked away.

Modern dairymen would scoff at a cow eating melon rinds, leftover salads, potato peelings, overripe fruit, pea pods, corn shucks, spaghetti. We fed garbage. One of our cows, Susie, liked meat.

This mixed diet didn't seem to offset the flavor of the milk much. We used our milk raw, but we used it very quickly. Milk was also kept scrupulously clean, not by modern standards, but by my mother's. Mother said she could see germs with the naked eye. When she poured the warm milk through a cheesecloth strainer, about all she got out were the frogs and the flies. But it looked clean and tasted fine.

We did have trouble with wild onions. In a big dairy, one cow with off-flavor milk probably doesn't affect the whole bulk-milk tank. When the herd is just one cow, and that cow is filled with wild onions, the milk is fit only for onion soup.

When a cow became mournful, we turned to *Bailey's* for her needs. *Bailey's Cyclopedia of Agriculture* isn't well known today, but we couldn't have done without it. . . . Many of *Bailey's* theories have since been disproved, but I suppose even a modern cow would respond to a good dose of salts, and *Bailey's* prescribed salts for almost everything.

Bailey's also spoke of what to do with a high molar. One of our first cows, Bessie, had such an affliction. It pained her and she wouldn't eat—not even molasses. I got her mouth propped open with a short broomstick and filed the tooth down with a wood rasp. It never bothered her again, thanks to *Bailey's*.

I wonder now why we never had *leptospirosis,* or *brucellosis,* or *acetonemia,* or *hemorrhagic septicemia,* or for that matter, *aftosa.* In later years we tested for TB, but we had few major health problems which we didn't cause ourselves with poor feed, poor hay, or irregular hours.

Milking and tending the cow were round-the-clock business. Up every morning before dawn all winter, to feed and milk, home for milking, feeding and bedding every night. Strangely enough, it wasn't unpleasant. There was always a half-hour of peace and quiet, morning and evening, to plan a day's work and to go over what had been done or learned or missed. I used my chore time to think, to conjure up football plays, to memorize parts in the school plays and to practice debate. Cows liked to hear me sing; at least they never complained. How often have I wished, since I have grown up, that I had a half-hour in the morning and a half-hour every night when I could depend on being alone and unbothered.

Chores seize on a boy and won't let go. I have little sentimentality about the good old days nor do I set great store in the adage about giving a boy a cow to keep him from crime's door.

I won't say that the youngsters today are headed straight for trouble because they haven't got a family cow. She came from whence no one knows; she played her little part; and now she's gone. Bless her memory.

EDUCATING AMERICA

In the days before carpools, computers, and big yellow buses, getting an education often meant three-mile treks through severe weather and completing homework by a flickering kerosene lamp. But with the help of "school wagons" and primers that offered a hefty dose of moral virtues and pieties, the children arrived at school just in time for their "readin', writin', and 'rithmetic" lessons.

The earliest "school buses" were actually horse-drawn school wagons whose driver sat inside with the children. In the early 1920s, the ride to school had evolved to resemble a large touring car. But the 1940s brought the familiar sight of the bright yellow bus and a national standard for school buses nationwide.

A school teacher and her students pose outside of their school for a class picture in the 1890s. Except for the lucky children who owned the horse, most students walked to school.

Near the end of the century, *Austin Palmer's Guide to Muscular Movement Writing* introduced a writing style that was much more simple and efficient and that stressed correct posture and pen holding. Students across the country finally had a uniform style of penmanship that was easy to learn and read. By 1920, ninety percent of all American schools were using the Palmer method.

In the early 1800s, knowledge of penmanship offered plowmen a chance to leave their hard labor behind. Penmanship exercises promoted by those such as Plat Roger Spencer and his Spencerian method were popular nationwide and produced elaborately embellished letters and graceful forms.

When William Holmes McGuffey wrote his seven volumes of text-books for young students, he had no idea that his work would one day be called "one of the most remarkable educational ventures of the nineteenth century." But *McGuffey's Eclectic Readers* would go on to shape the minds of generations of American school-children until the 1920s. In the days when textbooks were few, the Readers offered students information on not only grammar and reading but geography, history, poetry, and literature. To hold the chil-dren's attention, McGuffey's lessons were interspersed with pictures, rhymes, and stories, which first popularized such favorite verses as "Mary had a little lamb" and "Twinkle, twinkle little star."

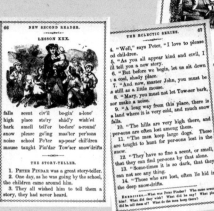

In the early 1930s, *Dick and Jane* primers became the educa-tional tool that no classroom could be without. Chronicling the simplistic adventures of Dick, Jane, Baby Sally, Mother, Father, Spot, and Puff, the books used repetition of one-syllable words to teach simple phrases. For four decades, public schools across the nation recognized the successful formula of the primers, which regularly outsold all their competition combined, and millions of American children could "See Jane run."

At the Philadelphia Centennial Exhibition of 1876, a novel con-cept for teaching was first intro-duced—building toys. One of the attendees was Mrs. Anna Wright, who ordered a set of the new kindergarten toys for her young son, future architect Frank Lloyd Wright. The blocks influenced not only young Frank but years later his own son, John Lloyd Wright, who was also an architect. In 1917, John was struck with an idea for a new toy. Ten minutes later, his concept was sketched on paper and he had named it Lincoln Logs, which became a favorite twenti-eth-century teaching toy.

THE SCHOOL

Edna Jaques

*A*t first, there was no school within fifteen miles of us. So dad thought that with four school-age kids running wild on the prairie, we must have a school. He drove to Moose Jaw and got in touch with the right people. I don't know how he did it, but one day we saw a wagon-load of lumber arrive in the yard with four men riding on it. They were the carpenters who had come to build a school. Dad took them to the place where the school was to be built, about a mile from our place.

I do not remember who donated the little half-acre for the school and yard, but next day Dad paced off the land (he was great at pacing land) and the foundations of the school were set down. I think the school was about twenty-by-forty—big enough to seat twenty kids. There were three windows on each side, a little plat-form at one end, a huge coal-burning stove at the back, and ten seats, two kids to a seat.

The first day there was great excitement

Two young girls enjoy their lunches; one has carried hers to school in a tin pail.

for everyone. Just thirteen kids showed up: among them were our four (Clyde, Edna, Madge, Arlie); Wyatts, two girls and a little boy; Mary and Bob Banks and their cousin, Lou Jacobs; Fred Elliot, and I don't remember the names of the rest. We were a shy bunch of kids, playing on top of a little pile of lumber, stealing glances at each other—suddenly shy at meeting for the first time.

We all walked to school, of course, carrying our lunches in shiny new lard pails; lunches usually consisted of a couple of slices of good homemade bread, hard-boiled eggs, and if we were lucky, a couple of cookies.

The Wyatt kids had to walk over three miles each way. Poor little Homer was just six, and his fat little legs were so tired that the minute he got into school he would go to sleep; the kindly teacher would just let him sleep, in the morning anyway.

The teacher was Miss Russel from Ottawa—a quiet, religious girl who read a chapter from the Bible before she gave us lessons; she seemed bewildered at the job she had got herself into. She didn't stay long. She was too gentle and shy for the new country and hated the hardship and cold and walking a mile to school at twenty below zero. . . .

Other teachers followed her, at about one per year. With the country filled with bachelor homesteaders, a new teacher was the talk of the country. "Did you see her? What does she look like? . . . Is she fat? . . . How tall is she?" But it wouldn't be long until they saw her for themselves. Some of them would call at the school with the pretext of looking for a lost horse, and ask her if she had seen it.

But she knew their tricks. Sometimes she would invite them in, put a chair for them on the platform, and go on with her work. Young fellows who never darkened the door of a church would come all spruced up, faces shining, hair slicked down, just to get a better look at the teacher.

Although this early school bus wasn't yellow, it offered a much more convenient trip than walking.

Teachers did well if they lasted a year. Half the country was filled with teachers. Girls from Ontario, New Brunswick, P.E.I., hunting for experience sure got it: forty below zero for weeks on end, blizzards that shut them in for days at a time, loneliness that almost drove them mad, and

Winslow Homer captures the simplicity of a one-room schoolhouse in his painting **The Country School.**

sometimes, after they were married, they had their babies without doctors or even neighbor women to help them.

I remember one whose baby started to come a cold winter day. Her husband started for Rouleau, fifteen miles away, to get a doctor; he had a team and a sleigh, but when he got halfway there a raging blizzard started up and poor Tom got lost and landed on a farm about fifteen miles from where he was headed.

For hours the mother cried and yelled as the pains became unbearable. They had a hired man, a young fellow from Scotland, shy as only a young Scotsman can be. He stood it as long as he could. Then washing his hands, and putting on a clean shirt, he went to her and said, "Look, Misses, I can't stand any more of your screaming. I am used to helping the mother lambs in Scotland when they're in trouble, so I'll help you." After the baby was born, he made the mother comfortable, washed and dressed the baby, and laid it

Country Schoolhouse

Do you have a little red schoolhouse
    safe in memory,
With an iron stove and an outside pump
    and a shady apple tree?

There were well-carved desks and a water pail
    and many shaggy books,
A round world globe, a few rough shelves . . .
    at the back, a row of hooks.

A long black stovepipe ran the length
    of the rudely finished room,
And a coal-oil lamp on a swinging chain
    helped dispel the gloom.

A blackboard graced the whole front wall;
    there was always lots of chalk.
You used a slate and your pencil squeaked,
    and no one dared to talk.

The modern schools are large and grand
    and beautiful to see,
But how many love the country school
    treasured in memory?

Helen E. Middleton

beside her, wrapped in a little white shawl.

When the blizzard died down, Tom came home almost afraid to come into the house. But there she was, sitting up in bed, everything cleaned up, having a cup of tea with her baby beside her. Poor Tom was so relieved, he kissed the hired man (before he kissed his wife or baby), and when the man was ready to go to his own homestead, Tom gave him a fine team of horses and helped him in a dozen different ways and was his friend as long as they lived.

THE COUNTRY DOCTOR

R. J. McGinnis

A product of an early Midwest medical school, he came to our little village in the hills of southern Ohio and hung out his shingle. His name was Alonzo Adams, and he was in his midtwenties. He grew a beard, and people were soon calling him "Old Doc," a name he carried for sixty years. He was the first doctor in our part of the country. Before he came we got along with a midwife, home remedies, and prayer. We survived. . . .

The cure for all ills was the brews and potions passed down from ancestors, and the old reliables, castor oil, Epsom salts, and arnica. They used whiskey and a wad of tobacco for disinfectant. Sulphur and molasses, followed by dandelion greens and sassafras tea, were sovereign spring remedies for phlegms accumulated in the body during the winter. Most ills were worn out, or they wore out the victim.

When a doctor came to a community he was promptly challenged by these home remedies, and Old Doc never quite conquered them. Naturally, he was called only when old home remedies failed and, of course, for accidents. He had to be wise and patient in substituting science for the bark of the sassafras root. He soon learned that he could not be a person, for there was really no place in the community for a person of his mythical and actual gifts. He was both at the top and the bottom of the social order, more important than the banker in time of trouble, less important than a hired hand when it came time to pay the bills. . . .

His fee for a house call was two dollars when he came to our community, and when he died sixty years later his fee was still two dollars. A house call might take him two blocks down the street on a pleasant summer afternoon; it might take him twenty miles into the country in the worst blizzard of the winter.

While Old Doc practiced his profession without the multitude of scientific refinements we have today, he did surprisingly well with his simple drugs and tools. He was a good diagnostician of the mind as well as the body, and was not above psychological tricks if he thought they were needed. He regularly sold, for a dime a bottle, "the best cure for sore throat in the country." It was a six-ounce bottle of common salt solution, colored red, and was used as a gargle. If asked what it was, Old Doc lowered his voice mysteriously and said, "Sodium chloride and H_2O."

He was versatile, too. He pulled teeth, examined the eyes for glasses, and occasionally ministered to a sick cow or horse. His favorite remedy was a vile mixture of quinine, iron, and strychnine, which he called Q.I.S. Sometimes calomel was substituted for the strychnine. It was a sort of shotgun mixture good for most anything that came along, could do no harm, and tasted vile enough to satisfy the most rabid hypochondriac. Most of the emergency surgery was performed in the field or on a kitchen table. His surgical kit contained a saw, two or three scalpels, a pair of forceps, and a needle with a length of catgut.

He might have laid by a fortune, for he never had time to spend money, if he collected only a modest percentage of what was owed him. . . . Old Doc was paid out of conscience money. He rarely collected his five-dollar fee for the birth of the first child; it was only after the second came along that the embarrassed father paid his old bill. He was paid in odd ways, too. The very poor were the best pay, for they put a bag of potatoes or a couple of fat hens in the boot of his buggy when he left, and often at Christmastime a ham or a barrel of apples came his way on a bill he long since had written off. He never billed his [debtors]. He never married; never, no time for courting.

Joe Wilson, some thirty-five years old and a well-to-do farmer, went to Old Doc for a birth certificate. He wanted to take his family to Europe and needed records for his passport. Old Doc looked up his records, wrote out the certificate and handed it to Joe. "How much do I owe you?" asked Joe. It was then that Old Doc came as near as he ever had come to dunning a [debtor]. "You don't owe me anything for the certificate," he said, "but you're not paid for yourself yet. Your father forgot the item when you were born."

Old Doc's sole heir was a nephew in Pittsburgh. He biggest legacy was six ledgers recording three score years of service and more than $100,000 in unpaid bills, some almost sixty years old. He left also a modest house in the village, 120 stony acres and an old farmhouse two miles out, and three old horses.

He kept two horses in a stable at the back of his home, a light cart for summer use, and a staunch, closed buggy for the bad season. People said he wore out a horse a year galloping over country roads in a sea of mud to bring a baby, or tie up an artery. His horses and the stable were cared for by the village dolt, Henry Carr, who slept in a room in the stable and was always on call. When Old Doc died, Henry got his bank account — $325.76.

Old Doc passed away during the peak of a flu epidemic. It was not the flu that took him, but at eighty-six, two days and nights without taking off his clothes and with no food except coffee was too much for his aging heart. He came in early one morning, fell asleep in his chair in his office, and never awakened. He has the finest marble monument in our cemetery, put up by his faithful friends who never thought to pay him in life, but opened their purses when he died. His funeral was the largest in the history of our village.

Before he came we got along with a midwife, home remedies, and prayer.

NORTH DAKOTA COOK

Carrie Young

y mother was fond of saying that anyone could be a fine cook if unlimited ingredients were available; to prepare tasty and attractive food with what one had on hand was the real challenge. If my gustative memories of childhood on the western plains serve me right—and they seem to become more salivary with the years—my mother and most of the other hardy young women of Norwegian descent who set up housekeeping in tiny homestead cabins in the early 1900s were more than up to the challenge.

When I think of the food of my childhood, I think first of holidays: of the *lutefisk* and *lefse*, of the delicately spicy Norwegian meatballs in gravy, of the nothing-but-butter cookies—the *sandbakkels*, the *spritz*, and the *berliner-kranzer*. I close my eyes and smell the breathtaking icy freshness of the hand-cranked ice cream on Christmas Eve. . . .

Then I think of harvesttime. I see the great threshing machine in a vast wheatfield of golden shocks of grain that stand out like miniature Indian tepees as far as the eye can sweep. . . . I see a dozen wagons piled high with sheaves lined up behind the threshing machine, the men perched up on the sheaves as they wait their turns to throw the bundles into the separator. . . . The faces of the men are covered with wheat chaff, and their lips stand out crimson from the irritation of the dust.

A moment later I see my mother in the kitchen. She is lining a large dish-pan with a snowy floursack dish towel and heaping it high with butter sandwiches and doughnuts. I see her standing over the black cast-iron range making coffee in a giant granite coffeepot, see her vigorously grinding the coffee at the hand grinder on the wall, see her mixing the ground coffee with an egg—shell and all—and dropping it into the pot, pouring boiling water over it, letting it settle, then pouring a cup of cream into it.

She lifts the coffeepot from the stove and walks out the door with it, trailed by my sisters Gladys and Fran carrying the dishpan between them and by my brother Norman carrying the tin pail full of cups. I tag along, barefoot, for the pure joy of it as they walk out to the threshing rig to serve the men their nine A.M. coffee break. Only we don't call it coffee break. We call it "forenoon lunch."

The men jump down from their wagons and squat on their haunches to form a circle around us. My mother pours the coffee into the thick white china cups and passes them around to the men. . . .

The men each take a sandwich or two, but they reach more eagerly for the doughnuts because my mother is a superb doughnut maker, having made at least enough of them in her lifetime to provide her with a chain link to heaven. They are firm and rich and deeply browned, ideal for dunking, and they will stick to a man's ribs until dinnertime. . . .

Workmen enjoy a harvest dinner prepared by a capable country cook.

We make a similar trip at four P.M., and we call this "afternoon lunch." There are, of course, also breakfast, dinner, and supper—which the men eat in the kitchen. At the 4:30 A.M. breakfast there are soda pancakes and fried eggs in butter with salt pork on the side. At dinner there are mountains of mashed potatoes, fried beefsteak, creamed carrots and peas, pickled beets, bread and butter, and my mother's famous lemon meringue pie. At supper there are American fried potatoes, cold sliced roast pork, scalloped macaroni and tomatoes, dill pickles, and my mother's renowned devil's food cake with rhubarb sauce. . . .

When I think of the food of my childhood, I

My mother's doughnuts will stick to a man's ribs until dinnertime.

never think of it as lacking in variety—a tribute to my mother's ingenuity. The two categories of food that were lacking on the prairies were fruits and vegetables. The growing season was much too short for fruit. Frost came too early in the fall and stayed too late in the spring. Oranges were rare items that appeared in our Christmas stockings. Apples were available only in the winter when they were shipped in from the West in bushel crates. And the only vegetable that would grow with certainty, year in and year out—even in the Dust Bowl years—were potatoes. In good years, carrots, peas, beets, onions, and cucumbers also grew well.

But the North Dakota soil seemed to be able to produce potatoes under any conditions.

When all else failed during the drought years, of which there were many, potatoes provided the homesteaders with an abundantly nutritious food—their only regular source of vitamin C. My mother often served potatoes twice a day. Far from tiring of them, I still love them so much that if I could choose one food to be marooned with on a desert island, I'd probably take potatoes. I'd take them boiled, baked, mashed, scalloped, or browned. But above all, I'd take them in my mother's potato salad.

One taste of my mother's potato salad and it was indelibly imprinted on your palate, leaving you forever immune to paler versions. To make the dressing, she put a dozen egg yolks in a saucepan, together with two cups of vinegar, two tablespoons of mustard, a tablespoon of salt, and a half cup of sugar. She cooked this mixture very slowly until it was thick, after which she beat in a couple of tablespoons of butter. After this had cooled, she added an equal amount, more or less, of thick sour cream, tasting and adding until she had the flavor just right. If she happened to have some new onions in the garden, she snipped off a few green tops, diced them, and added them. My mother's potato salad was so savory that there was seldom any

left over on the second day, but if there was, it was so zingy that one dish of it would float you to the ceiling, where, suspended, you were quite willing to die happy. . . .

The sharing of food was a way of life on the prairies. It was shared with joy and laughter in health and with love and concern in time of illness. A case in point is the famous incident of my mother's chicken soup. The time was the harsh winter of the great influenza epidemic in 1919. My mother already had three children under the age of five and another under the apron. As the flu raged across the country, farm families in the community quarantined themselves. The men went to town only to replenish essential supplies. But late in March, when the winter blizzards were at their worst, my father came down with a severe case of the flu and was bedridden. My mother had to milk the cows as well as feed and water the horses and other livestock. The pump at the windmill kept freezing up, and she had to pour boiling water down the casing to thaw the ice. It was a desperate time.

One day the mail carrier, who was the only outside contact my mother had, told her that her cousin Tomas's family, who lived a mile down the road, had also been struck with the flu. Ingeborg, the mailman reported, had been flat

A bountiful crop was a farmer's reward.

A farmhouse stands amid an Oregon prairie.

the chicken soup and suddenly became so ravenously hungry that she sat up in bed, seized the jar, and drank deeply.

It was the first nourishment she had been able to swallow for days. From that moment on she gained strength and soon was well.

A robust woman with a ringing laugh, Ingeborg was a marvelous storyteller, and by the time I was born and had grown old enough to hear the story, it had already become a classic. Each time Ingeborg told the story, she drank more of the soup than the time before. When she had recounted the story for twenty years, she was consuming the entire half gallon at once!

on her back for ten days and was getting weaker and weaker because she could swallow neither food nor water.

My mother anguished for a way in which she could help. She did what she could do. She went out to the chicken coops and managed to catch two roosters, chopped their heads off, cleaned and boiled them, and made a rich chicken soup. She poured it into a half-gallon canning jar and sealed it. Then she went out to the barn, harnessed up a pair of horses, hitched them to the box sled, and drove over the snow-packed roads to her neighbors' farm. She pressed the jar of chicken soup into Tomas's hands, turned the horses around, and hurried home to her family.

Now Ingeborg takes over the telling of the story. Ingeborg reported that when her husband came to the bedroom with the jar of soup and lifted off the lid, she smelled the aroma of

Prairie Born

I'm lonesome for the old trails
That wound across the plain,
The willows by the coulee's rim
That swished against the rain.
For cattle bawling in the night,
The coyote's lonely cry,
For sage and buffalo willow smoke
Drifting to the sky.

I want the little sounds once more
That common folk like me
Were raised to love and listen for,
The droning of a bee.
And cattle feeding on the range
The first pale light of morn,
I'm going back where I belong,
For I am prairie born.

Edna Jaques

HOMEGROWN GOODNESS

Country cooks were often forced to be innovative and rely on whatever crops the fields, gardens, and weather yielded. But the family was richly rewarded by enjoying the freshest, most colorful foods prepared according to treasured family recipes that could satisfy the hungriest of appetites.

CARAMELIZED FRIED GREEN TOMATOES (Serves 4)

4 large green tomatoes
1 cup yellow cornmeal
1½ teaspoons salt

2 teaspoons freshly ground pepper
Vegetable oil for frying
4 tablespoons brown sugar

Slice tomatoes into rounds about ½ inch thick. Combine cornmeal, salt, and pepper in a pie plate. Press tomato slices into the mixture, turning to coat both sides. In a large skillet, heat oil over medium heat. When hot, add tomatoes and fry until browned, about 5 minutes. Turn over and sprinkle brown sugar over tops. When second side is browned, carefully turn tomatoes, sugared side face down. Cook for about 1 minute and, while cooking, sprinkle a little brown sugar over what are now the tops. Flip them over one more time and cook the second sides just long enough to caramelize the sugar, about 1 minute more. Serve hot.

CORN RELISH (Makes 6 pints)

16 ears corn or enough to make 8 cups fresh
    corn kernels
4 cups chopped cabbage
1 quart white vinegar
1½ cups granulated sugar
1 cup water
1 cup chopped sweet red bell pepper

1 cup chopped green bell pepper
1 cup chopped onion
2 tablespoons ground mustard
1 tablespoon salt
1 tablespoon celery seed
1 tablespoon ground turmeric

In a large pot, bring to a boil enough water to cover corn; drop corn in and boil 5 minutes. Drain corn and cut from cobs. In the pot, combine corn with remaining ingredients. Simmer 20 minutes. Bring to a boil, stirring constantly. Ladle into hot, sterilized pint jars within ½ inch of the top of jar. Adjust caps; process 15 minutes in a boiling water bath. (Start counting processing time when water returns to a boil.) Remove jars and allow to cool before storing.

SWEET GREEN BEAN PICKLES (Makes 3 pints)

1½ to 2 pounds green beans, trimmed
2 cups cider vinegar
⅓ cup granulated sugar
1½ tablespoons mixed pickling spices, tied in a
    cheesecloth bag
1 tablespoon whole black peppercorns

1 bay leaf
1 clove garlic
1 large onion, chopped
1 small red bell pepper, seeded and chopped
3 large sprigs dill

Bring a pot of salted water to a boil; add beans and blanch for 1 minute. Drain and rinse under cold running water. Drain well. In a medium saucepan, combine vinegar, sugar, pickling spices, peppercorns, bay leaf, and garlic. Bring to a boil; reduce heat and simmer 10 minutes. Remove bay leaf and garlic. Pack beans upright in sterilized jars (up to 1 inch from the top). With a slotted spoon, divide the onions and red peppers evenly among the jars. Place a dill sprig in each jar and pour in hot syrup up to ½ inch from the top. Seal the jars. Process in a hot water bath for 15 minutes.

BUTTERNUT SQUASH (Serves 6)

1 3-pound butternut squash, peeled, seeded,
    and cut into 1-inch cubes
⅛ teaspoon salt
    Freshly ground pepper

1 apple, peeled, cored, and chopped
1 teaspoon honey
1 tablespoon fresh lemon juice
⅛ teaspoon grated nutmeg

In a large saucepan, bring ½ cup water to a boil. Add squash, salt and pepper and cover. Return to a boil. Cook squash until it is tender, about 3 minutes. Add apple; cover and cook an additional 2 minutes. Drain and remove squash and apple to a serving dish. Mix together honey and lemon juice and drizzle over the squash and apple. Sprinkle with nutmeg and serve.

FARM-STYLE KALE (Serves 4)

2 strips bacon
1 tablespoon butter
1 small onion, finely chopped
1 pound kale, washed, stems removed
    and chopped

Salt and pepper
Pinch of ground allspice
1 tablespoon red wine vinegar
1 lemon, thinly sliced

In a large skillet, fry bacon until crisp. Drain on paper towels. Crumble and set aside. Add butter to the bacon drippings. Add onion and cook over medium-low heat until golden. Add kale with just the water that clings to the leaves. Cover and cook, stirring occasionally, until tender, about 15 minutes. Add salt and pepper to taste, allspice, and vinegar. Toss and turn out into a serving dish. Sprinkle with the reserved bacon and garnish with lemon slices.

CHRISTMAS IN THE WOODS

Louise Dickinson Rich

Christmas in the woods is much better than Christmas on the Outside. We do exactly what we want to do about it. . . . We don't have any synthetic pre-Christmas build-up—no shop window displays, no carol singers in department stores, no competition in the matter of lighting effects over front doors. . . . We didn't even have a Santa Claus until last year. We thought it would be nice if Rufus grew up knowing who gave him presents and bestowing his gratitude in the proper places. So we had never even mentioned the name of You-know-who. However, a visitor at Millers let him in on the secret, explaining to him that Santa Claus is the man who brings things for little boys. Rufus knew very well that Larry Parsons brings in everything we get from the Outside. Q.E.D., Larry is Santa Claus. He still persists in this belief, which makes him perfectly happy and we hope it does Larry, too.

We don't even have a Christmas tree. It seems a little silly, with hundreds of square miles of fir and spruce, from knee-high babies to giants of eighty feet on all sides of us, to cut one down and bring it into the house. It seems almost like vandalism to shake the ice and snow from its branches and hang them with popcorn strings and cheap tinsel. We have our Christmas tree outdoors, for the benefit of the birds, hanging suet and crusts on the branches of one of the trees in the yard.

But we do have Christmas, just the same, and since we are so far from stores and last minute shopping, we have to start planning for it a long time ahead. With no chance to shop for gadgets, we have to make quite a lot of our presents, and the rest we get from what is known here simply as the Mail Order. I give mittens, handmade by me with the initials of the recipient knit into the design across the back. These don't cost much over and above my time, and no one in this country ever had too many pairs of mittens. For people who live Outside I try to think up things that they couldn't buy in stores. After all, it would be simple-minded to send out and buy something, have it mailed in here, wrap it up, and send it out to someone who, doubtless, lives almost next door to the store where it was bought.

I make little mittens about an inch long and sew them onto a bright fourteen-inch length of cord, as children's mittens are sewed onto a cord. These are bookmarks, in case you haven't guessed. To city people who, I know, have fireplaces, I send net bags full of the biggest and best pinecones I can find, to be

We have our Christmas tree outdoors, for the benefit of the birds, hanging suet and crusts on the branches.

used as kindling. I make balsam pillows. . . . I collect old-fashioned patchwork quilt patterns from any source I can find them, and use them to make my pillow covers. In the old quilts, each unit is usually from twelve to fifteen inches square, and that makes a very good size for a balsam pillow. I make them, naturally, by hand, and they look very simple and expensive. They don't cost very much either. And I do love the names of the old patterns—Star of Bethlehem, Wedding Ring, Flower Garden, Log Cabin. They have a nice homely sound. You can think of a lot of things to make out of nothing, if you have to.

But making presents isn't half of Christmas in the woods. I'll never forget the year the lake didn't even begin to freeze until well after the tenth of December. We'd ordered our Mail Order, and presumably the Andover Post Office was harboring our stuff until someone could go out to get it. Finally, the day before Christmas, it was decided that an expedition should go on foot, get the stuff, and then, if at all possible considering the thin ice, drive it all in in Larry's old Model T which was down at the Arm.

We had living with us then a friend named Rush Rogers. He and Ralph and Edward Miller and Arch Hutchins, who was working for Larry, joined forces and set off down the ice on foot dragging a couple of sleds behind them to haul the stuff in on if the ice proved unsafe for the car. They got to the Arm all right, and from there into Andover was easy in Miller's Outside car.

Sure enough, all our stuff—we'd sold a story a short while before and were having a fat Christmas that year—was at the Post Office. In fact, since the Post Office was small and space at a premium during the rush season, our packages were all piled in the front window like a display, and the population of Andover was standing outside guessing at their contents. The Middle Dam delegation continued on to Rumford, stocked up with groceries and Christmas Cheer, picked up the mail and packages on the way back, and arrived back at the Arm in the afternoon. The mail and supplies filled the Ford to bulging. Arch wedged himself into

Memory cannot forget such a majestic scene.

the driver's seat, Edward stood on the running board to watch the high-piled packages, and Rush and Ralph tied the two sleds behind in single file and sat on them. I wish I could have seen them. The sleds were hardly big enough to accommodate their rears, and they had to hunch their knees up under their chins and hang on with both hands for dear life. Arch was driving the old Ford as fast as it would go, snow and ice chips from the chains were flying into their faces, so they couldn't keep their eyes open, and the sleds at the ends of their lines were slewing with terrific swoops.

Although this car likely cost over eight hundred dollars new, its productivity in snowy weather was quite limited.

As a final touch they held their bare hunting knives in their teeth so they could cut the sleds loose if the car went through the ice ahead of them. Edward told me later that they were the funniest-looking rig he ever saw.

The ice was really too thin to be safe. It bent and bowed under the weight of the car, and rolled up ahead of them in long flexible swells. But Arch followed the rules for driving a car on thin ice—keep the doors open, go like the wind, and be ready to jump—and they got home all right, only a little late for supper.

Then started one of the most hectic evenings I have ever spent. First, everything had to be unpacked; and when the Mail Order packs, it packs, what I mean. Corrugated board, excelsior, paper padding—they certainly give it the works. We decided that Ralph would do the unpacking in the back bedroom, with no lamp. He could see enough by the light through the open door. We didn't want any fire on Christmas Eve, and all that packing material around loose was definitely a fire hazard. Rush would assemble all of Rufus' toys that came knocked down—and that year most of them did—but first he had to put the new batteries, which were in the mess somewhere, into the radio so I could hear the Christmas carols.

I would re-wrap packages prettily. I started out with our present to Renny Miller, a five-cell flashlight, which we thought might come in handy for him. A flashlight is an awkward thing to wrap neatly, but I did a fairly good job and went on to the next thing. Rush was back of the chimney doing something to the radio wires, and in a minute he said, "Hey, Louise, where's that flashlight of Renny's? Lemme have it a second, will you?" I unwrapped, let him have it a second, and wrapped it up again.

I'd barely got the bow tied satisfactorily

when a yelp came from the back room, "Good-night, there goes a box of blocks! Hey, Louise, lemme have that flashlight of Renny's a second, will you?" I unwrapped it, let Ralph have it a second, and wrapped it up again. The back bedroom, I noted in passing, looked as if a brisk breeze had swept through it. I wrapped up the snow gliders we'd got for the two younger Miller children and looked around for Rush. He had disappeared, so this looked like the opportune time to tie up the mittens I'd made him,

A sleigh ride was not only fun, but often offered the only means of transportation during the hardest days of winter.

and the checked wool shirt that was Ralph's present to him. I got out a suitable piece of Christmas paper and some silver cord.

Then came a rapping on the window, and in the glow of the lamplight I saw Rush's face, framed in icicles and spruce branches. He didn't look like Father Christmas, though. He looked like a man in distress. "Hey, Louise, I can't see a thing out here by this aerial. Bring out that flashlight of Renny's a minute, will you?" I unwrapped it again—carefully, this time, as the paper was getting a little shabby at the creases—and took it out. In passing through the back room I observed that the brisk breeze had risen to gale velocity. I could still see the top of the bureau and of Ralph, but the bed had been drifted under. I held the flashlight while Rush did whatever he had to do. We went back into the house and turned on the radio. A very satisfactory rendition of "Holy Night" rewarded us. I re-wrapped Renny's present, decided it looked pretty moth-eaten, undid it, got fresh paper and ribbon, and did it up again.

As "Holy Night" changed to "Oh, Little Town of Bethlehem," I listened with pleasure, wrapping up presents, while Rush started to put together Rufus' bounce horse. When the music came to an end, I woke up to the fact that Ralph had been shouting for some time from the back room. "Hey, Louise! Bring that flashlight of Renny's!"

Before we went to bed that night I had wrapped that flashlight nine times. I had become a much better flashlight wrapper by midnight than I had been at seven o'clock.

At midnight we had some sherry and crackers and cheese. Because this was Christmas, Ralph had a raw egg in his sherry—which I think is barbarous—and Rush brought me a magnificent treat—Camembert cheese, which Ralph considers equally barbarous. We were exhausted and silly and we had a lot of fun. It was the best Christmas Eve I ever had, in spite of the flashlight.

MAIL-ORDER WISHES

Near the turn of the century, approximately sixty-five percent of the American population still lived in rural areas and relied on the familiar general store for almost all their purchases. But the stores' high prices and limited choices prompted consumers to turn to a new concept: shopping by mail. The institution of rural free mail delivery in 1896 and parcel post in 1913 fueled the new catalog industry and made local shopping unnecessary. Rural customers could now order everything from chickens to a new house just by browsing through their "wish books," delivered courtesy of the U.S. mail.

The first mail-order catalog, a flyer listing 163 items, was produced by Chicago-based Montgomery, Ward and Company and sent to members of the country's largest farm organization, the National Grange. The flyer was an immediate success among tens of thousands of farmers who appreciated the company's pledge of "satisfaction guaranteed, or your money back."

In 1886, Richard Sears, a Chicago railway station agent, began selling watches at a profit to other station agents up and down the line. After his endeavor was a success, he teamed up with watchmaker Alvah C. Roebuck, and the two twenty-somethings formed the mail-order company Sears, Roebuck and Co. Offering a happy alternative to the high-priced rural stores, the Sears catalog was the answer to farmers' prayers. By the turn of the century, the catalog had more than five hundred pages and sold everything from saddles to baby carriages to a Stradivarius model violin priced at $6.10.

As the smoke from World War I cleared in the early 1920s, consumer purchasing power boomed, and Sears, Roebuck and Co. planned to ride the crest. Sears had already offered the American people everything from automobiles to groceries, and now it would offer completely prefabricated houses as well. Catalogs pictured a wide spectrum of homes and touted the benefits of "ready-cut" lumber that was labeled for easy assembly. By the early 1930s, when the Depression put an end to the market, more than one hundred thousand families had chosen their homes out of a Sears, Roebuck catalog of houses.

W. Atlee Burpee was one of the bright entrepreneurs who saw nothing but opportunity in the new rural mail delivery. He first planned to use the mail-order business to sell the fancy purebred poultry he raised; but he quickly realized that his customers were more interested in purchasing seeds for animal feed, vegetables, and flowers (seeds that the catalog had offered as a courtesy) than livestock. Burpee began producing free catalogs whose humorous prose, testimonial letters, and colorful engravings made them a pleasure to read. By 1915, Burpee was the largest mail-order seed business in the world, and gardeners nationwide anticipated each new catalog's tips from the one-time poultry-breeder.

Trips, Trains, and a Model T:
MEMORIES OF GOING PLACES

Memories of Afar

Ideal vacations always end
In lovely memories;
When souvenirs have long been lost,
The heart remembers these.

The mountains reaching to the sky
Half hidden in a cloud;
The stalwart pines along their sides
So stately, tall and proud.

The rocky shore one stood upon
As day drew to a close
To watch the sunset tint the sea
In tones of gold and rose.

The friendly smiles and greetings that
One met in ev'ry town;
The hillsides turned by autumn's touch
To russet, gold, and brown.

The babbling brook that led one to
A mossy, wooded glen;
The perfect peace that one found there
And often sought again.

No photograph or souvenir
Can ever quite impart
The warmth such mem'ries kindle in
The confines of the heart.

Peggy Mlcuch

Artists Currier and Ives capture the glory days of the railroad in their painting The Express Train.

THE PICNIC TO THE HILLS

Edna Jaques

The picnic to the hills was the highlight of the summer. We always held it on the first of July. It was the only outing of the year. I couldn't sleep a wink the night before; I would just lie there in bed with my little sister, getting up a dozen times to look out the little narrow window and see if it was getting daylight, maybe drop off to sleep for a few minutes and then spring up again and see dawn coming up across the flats. And there is no more glorious sight on this earth than the sun slowly rising on the prairie, filling the summer world with colors that defy description. . . .

Meadow larks would be piping their songs. . . . The rooster would let out a few squawks; the dog would shake himself and wander toward the barn, as if to reassure himself that all was well; the hens would come out . . . ruffling their wings and start to hunt for food. The old cow on her tether would rise and stretch and start to eat as if to say, "Well, get up everyone. It's another day."

By this time we three girls would be dressed. There were no "outfits" for us, just nice little print dresses, the good ones we had been saving for the occasion.

We could hear Dad in the kitchen making the fire, cussing a bit under his breath and yelling at Maw to hurry.

Breakfast would be a hurried meal: good oatmeal porridge, big slices of homemade bread with syrup, and homemade butter. Dad and the boys would each eat a big slice of fried pork. Maw would have her tea; there was no tea for kids in those days, just milk or water gulped down in a hurry for fear we'd miss something.

My mother would have made most of the lunch the night before and packed in the blue bread pan: homemade head cheese, potato salad, radishes and little green onions, and maybe a bit of leftover Christmas cake, a raisin pie and her good homemade cookies.

Old Kit and Farmer would be hitched to the lumber wagon with dad and maw on the spring seat, we three in the back of the wagon as usual, laughing and wild with excitement. As the hills would loom nearer, we would see a few trees, our first glimpse of them since the picnic the year before.

The trail headed due south, winding here and there with a little curve around a gopher or badger hole, past Gallaugher's, Fraser's, Espelein's, where there was a tiny coulee to cross. Dad would ease the horses down the little bank and splash through the creek, maybe two feet of water in it, and then up the far bank, the horses flopping and scrambling for a foothold as if we were crossing the river Jordan.

Ahead, the hills would beckon, rising blue and lovely against the sky; the horses would trot along quietly as if they too were enjoying the break from the prairie and the plow.

My two brothers, Bruce and Clyde, would ride their horses; no wagon for them. Now and then they would pass us at a gallop, then circle back and race away again, leaving a little cloud of dust that settled down on the sage bushes and short grass, described by the oldtimers as "prairie wool."

Our destination would be "old Buchanan's ranch," exactly twelve miles south of our homestead. He would come out to meet us with his dog, smiling and glad to see another human being, I suppose.

The ranch cattle and horses, hearing us come, would get on top of the hill behind the house and view us from afar, half afraid. There were trees there, real trees that we only saw once a year. My mother would almost cry and go over and pat them. And I know now how utterly homesick she must have been for the sight of a tree, and the smell of the leaves in her hand.

We kids would run up and down the little hills, tripping and falling and wild with joy just to be able to run up a hill. We'd take a drink of water from

"Buchanan's spring" which was known all over the country as being the sweetest water on earth. How good it was, after the alkali water from our well or sloughwater with wigglers in it.

Dad would build a little fire to make tea, and we'd invite Mr. Buchanan to eat with us. They'd laugh and talk together.

For the first year or so there would be just us and two or three other families, but soon more settlers would join in and within five or six years there would be maybe fifty people out. Not many, I know, but fifty people in a new country was wonderful. The women would talk and laugh and compare notes on setting hens and new calves, and discuss how good it was to get out and talk to someone besides themselves.

Then it would be time to "hit for home" in the blue dusk of day, everyone quieter; we three kids in the back of the wagon were happy too, to be going home.

Toots, the dog, would come out to meet us,

Turn-of-the-century friends enjoy a riverside picnic.

smiling, I swear, to see us back. The house and barn looked strangely comfortable in the quiet dusk—the cows waiting to be milked, the hens to be fed and their water pans filled up again. Then quietness would settle down and fold us in, as if the earth too was glad we were home safe and sound.

FOOD FOR THE ROAD

During the hottest days of the summer, there was no better family fun than piling in the car, driving to the country, and spending a lazy afternoon on a red-and-white-checkered cloth under a large shade tree. The picnic basket always seemed to hold an endless supply of tasty treats, from lemonade to fried chicken, perfect for enjoying between games of tag or croquet.

BUTTERMILK CRISPY FRIED CHICKEN (Serves 6)

2 2½-pound frying chickens
   Salt and pepper to taste
1 cup buttermilk
1½ cups all-purpose flour
2 teaspoons paprika
1½ cups vegetable shortening

Remove excess fat and skin from chicken pieces and trim off the ends of the wings. Rinse pieces and pat dry with paper towels. In a large mixing bowl, place the chicken pieces. Sprinkle with salt and pepper. Pour buttermilk over the chicken and place in the refrigerator for 30 minutes. In a large plastic bag, combine flour, paprika, and salt and pepper to taste. Heat shortening in a large, heavy skillet over medium-high heat until hot but not smoking. Remove the chicken pieces from the buttermilk a few at a time, and place them into the bag of flour. Shake the bag gently to coat all sides. Remove the chicken from the flour, shaking off excess, and gently place it in the oil, skin side down. Fry the chicken pieces about 15 to 20 minutes on each side, then turn and cook other side. When chicken is golden brown on all sides, remove and drain on paper towels. Store in refrigerator.

PICNIC POTATO SALAD (Makes about 8 servings)

4 to 5 large russet potatoes
½ cup diced celery
½ cup diced red bell pepper
⅓ cup chopped sweet pickles
2 tablespoons minced red onion
4 hard-boiled eggs, chopped
1 cup mayonnaise
1 teaspoon spicy mustard
1 tablespoon red wine vinegar
   Salt and pepper to taste

Boil potatoes until tender, but not mushy. Drain and remove skins. When cool, cut into ½-inch cubes. In a large bowl, combine pota-toes, celery, bell pepper, sweet pickles, onion, and eggs. Toss to mix; set aside. In a small bowl, combine mayonnaise, mustard, vinegar, and salt and pepper to taste; mix well. Pour over potato mixture and fold in with a rubber spatula. Cover and chill about 4 hours. *Note*: When taking to a picnic, keep this salad cold. Discard salad if it has been left unrefrigerated for more than 30 minutes.

OLD-FASHIONED PEACH ICE CREAM (Makes ½ gallon)

2 pounds fresh, ripe peaches
1 tablespoon freshly squeezed lemon juice
¾ cup granulated sugar, divided
3 cups whipping cream
1 cup whole milk
1 tablespoon vanilla
4 egg yolks

Peel, pit, and slice the peaches. In a large bowl, combine peach slices with lemon juice and ¼ cup of the sugar. Toss well to coat all slices; set aside. In a heavy saucepan, combine cream, milk, ½ cup sugar, and vanilla. Cook and stir over medium heat until milk is hot but not boiling and the sugar is dissolved. Remove from heat. In a small bowl, beat egg yolks slightly. While constantly whisking egg yolks with a wire whisk, drizzle 1 cup of hot milk mixture into the yolks until smooth. Pour the yolk mixture into the hot milk mixture, whisking constantly. Heat over medium heat about 6 to 8 minutes, stirring constantly, until mixture coats the back of a spoon. Cool to room temperature. Strain into a bowl and mash peaches. Stir peaches into the custard mixture and freeze in an ice cream maker according to manufacturer's instructions.

OLD-FASHIONED RAISIN PIE (Makes one 9-inch pie)

Pastry for a double-crust pie
1 cup packed brown sugar
2 tablespoons cornstarch
2 cups raisins
½ teaspoon orange zest
½ teaspoon lemon zest
½ cup fresh orange juice
2 tablespoons fresh lemon juice
1⅓ cups cold water
½ cup chopped walnuts

Preheat oven to 375° F. Prepare pastry. Roll out half into a 10-inch circle and place into a 9-inch pie pan, fluting edges. Set aside. In a large saucepan, combine brown sugar and cornstarch; stir until smoothly mixed. Add raisins, orange and lemon zest, orange and lemon juice, and cold water. Cook over medium heat, stirring constantly, until thickened. Cook and stir 1 additional minute. Remove from heat and stir in walnuts. Pour into prepared crust. Roll out remaining pastry and place on top of filling. Seal and flute edge. Cover edge with aluminum foil. Bake 40 minutes, removing foil during last half of baking time. Bake until crust is golden and filling is bubbly.

A Lizzie,
My Love and You

Marjorie Holmes

When I was a very little girl, the woman who actually drove an automobile was a rare and dashing creature. In fact an auto or "machine" was at one time a novel and impressive thing. My Grandfather Holmes was fond of recalling the day Uncle Frank telephoned to announce that he was driving out to the farm in a "machine." Neighbors listening in on the party line were so excited they phoned the news to anybody else who might have missed it, and lined up beside the country road to await his arrival. . . .

Cars soon became a common sight around town, although owned mostly by the privileged, such people as doctors, judges, and bankers; farmers were beginning to buy Flivvers, or Tin Lizzies, as the first Fords were called. You almost never saw a horse and buggy, although horse-drawn wagons were hitched up on side streets where the mealy-smelling feed stores stood. And "The Iceman Cometh" still meant the jingle of harness and the slow clop of hooves, while the milkman, the junk man, and a few of the delivery wagons from the grocery stores depended upon the horse to draw their simple cargo up the sunny alleys and along the shady streets. And the squeak of leather, the creak of wooden wheels, the rich vinegar tang of horseflesh and the sound of thick teeth wrenching grass were a part of childhood itself, warmly sweet and enthralling.

"But how did you *get* places?" my offspring demand.

"We walked," I tell them. "Ever hear of it? We used our feet."

For a vast network of sidewalks encompassed every small town. And everybody used them. To children, particularly, those sidewalks were a constant source of interest and concern. "Step on a crack you break your mother's back." You raced each other madly to the corners where the "good lucks" were (the imprint of a builder's name) and stamped on them. Sidewalks held seed pods to be squirted in the spring, and were rich with gold and scarlet leaves in the fall. In summer some were so hot to your bare feet you had to walk on the cool, tickling grass. In winter you slid joyously on the icy ones—against parental warnings about wearing out your shoes. Brothers were always having to shovel snowy sidewalks, girls being sent forth with brooms to sweep them. The condition of the sidewalk going past your house was of vast concern to mothers.

Mine always contended that "a slovenly sidewalk is the first sign of a slovenly house." . . .

Adults also depended on the sidewalks. Men walked to work in the morning and walked home for big boiled dinners at noon. And after the dishes were done and the dishtowels were drying on the back porch, their wives got dressed up and walked to Tuesday Club or Missionary Society or Ladies Aid. Whole families walked downtown to the movies after supper, or to the band concert in Sunset Park on Sunday afternoon. Boys walked girls home from church or library, and young couples strolled romantically along the lakeshore in the moonlight, arms entwined.

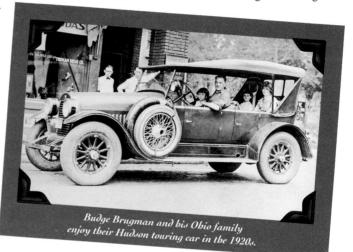

Budge Brugman and his Ohio family enjoy their Hudson touring car in the 1920s.

We lived quite near the lake; and like the child in Stevenson's poem I often lay reluctant to go to sleep, hearing that poignant preview to life itself—"The grown-up people's feet—still going by me on the street."

But more and more it became the cars going by. Oh, those lucky ones, those divinely favored—the peoplewho owned cars! My grandparents had moved to town by now and possessed a handsome Hudson touring car, although neither of them drove it. The chauffeuring was done by Aunt Ada, who had learned some years before by simply going down to the garage where Uncle Frank stored his "machine" and informing the men there that he had sent her for it. She was a school teacher, dazzlingly beautiful. Although no woman in the

entire county had ever been known to drive, the combination overpowered them. Whatever their misgivings, they cranked it up, flung open the doors, and watched her go bouncing off. When Uncle Frank sauntered in shortly thereafter and learned what had happened, they all paled. "You fools, if she kills herself I'll sue you!" Instead, she returned elated. One of them was so relieved he rushed off to be sick.

Aunt Ada took Grandmother out riding almost every day, and on rare and signal occasions they would invite us. To go for a ride with anybody was a big treat, but with Grandma it was positively awesome. She dressed in crackling taffeta and lacy shawls, and the diamonds in her ears sparkled like Aunt Ada's wit. We were almost too dazzled to enjoy it.

It was fitting that Grandma and Grandpa have a Golden Wedding. Not many people lived that long, and the whole town helped celebrate.

Their twelve children arrived from far-flung places and brought them a solid-gold pitcher and tray with twelve golden goblets. There was a feast worthy of Belshazzar. Most impressive of all was the fact that Aunt Barbara's family, who had vast holdings on the west coast, had driven clear across country by car! And what a car—the first sedan most of us had ever seen. With its tasseled window shades and cut-glass bud vases—

A mother poses with her children in front of the family's new Packard.

a veritable limousine. To ride in it was to positively wallow in reflected glory.

Oh, to own a car. Just any kind of car, like practically everybody else was getting. It wouldn't have to be a Dodge or an Overland or a Hupmobile; a Ford would be just dandy. How we envied the tourists who poured through town, camping by the lakeshore. . . . Traveling! To cross state lines, head for distant and exotic places like the Badlands of South Dakota or even Yellowstone park. Sometimes the cars flaunted self-kidding signs: CALIFORNIA OR BUST! The daring, the wonder—for they must climb mountains, brave deserts—and breakdowns and flat tires were accepted hazards among these knowing pioneers.

Storm Lake people, too, set off on these fabulous journeys, with luggage strapped to the fenders, tents roped on top, and the cheers and jokes of envious stay-at-homes in their ears. And to witness such a departure and only turn back to the humming blue haze of your own dumb yard was to suffer a consuming ache, a wild inchoate longing that could only be appeased by wheels.

And then Dad bought a car. I lay awake straining to hear him discussing the possibility with Mother one night, and praying. And the thrill when he actually came driving up in it for her to look over cannot be conveyed. It was, to be sure, a Lizzie, and secondhand. But its black tin sides were shiny, its canvas top a trifle imperious, propped high on its skinny arms. He sprang out jauntily, cap on the back of his head, face aglow. "Well, Mama, what d'you think?"

She was startled and timorous. "Oh, Sam, I've been wondering, can we really afford it?" (They were still paying on the note at the bank for his share of the solid-gold goblets.) "And—can you *drive* it?"

"Drive it? Can I *drive* it?" He threw back his head and laughed. Can birds fly? Can fish swim? Like most of his big rollicking family, he had been born knowing how to do grand, magnificent things. He strolled around it, fondly kicked a tire. The way he figured it, he told her, a traveling salesman almost had to have a car. This way he'd actually save money, not have to stay in hotels so often. He could get home lots more nights to be with the family. He hugged her and sniffed, in a little way he had, at her heavy black hair. They were very much in love, a fact of which we were blissfully unconscious, though it enriched our lives. What he was really telling her was that he could be home with her more often.

"Get in, come on, I'll take you for a spin."

"Oh, my goodness, I look a sight! Wait!" She hurried into the house to put on hat, coat and gloves, though it was a warm day. Meanwhile, half the neighborhood came running, thunderstruck. Kids swarmed all over the hot, leathery smelling upholstery, begging to go too, and of course to sit in the front seat. But no, that was reserved for Mother. Dad elegantly handed her in. She sat stiff and pale while he cranked up. Yank. Yank. Yank. A ferocious and seemingly futile undertaking.

Still emanating optimism, he trudged back, leaned inside to adjust the spark lever, pull the choke. More earnest jerks of the handle that protruded in front like an impudent tongue. He was beginning to perspire, and so was Mother in her Sunday best. She implored him not to strain himself. She could see on his pinkening face the gritting of teeth and tightening of lips that presaged an oath. Instead, he paused, mopping his brow, and lifting one side of the radiator, made mysterious adjustments within. Then, pressing bodily against his adversary, he gave the crank his all. Victory came with a few gasps, a mighty throat clearing, a roar so thunderous Dad had to leap aside. We all held on while he rushed around, vaulted in, yanking at levers, stepping on pedals, releasing brakes. We were off, down the shady streets of morning, with neighbors looking up from gardens and clotheslines to remark our triumphant departure. And Dad, to Mother's distress, further shattered the peace by loudly honking the rubber horn.

Whenever Dad was home there was no greater pleasure than to clamber into that dusty chariot and go for a ride. Mother often adjured

Traveling! To cross state lines, head for distant and exotic places like the Badlands of South Dakota or even Yellowstone Park. . . .

us not to tease. "Dad's tired, he's been driving all week, remember." But he was always a good sport about it. We drove along the familiar streets and parks that flanked the lake. We drove past the canning factory. Sometimes we drove to Alta, a neighboring town, and stopped for ice-cream cones. Sometimes, if we teased hard, we drove clear to Aurelia or Cherokee, beyond it. The gravel road pinged and crunched beneath the tires; the wind tore gloriously through as we sped along at the insane speed of thirty-five miles an hour.

"Now, Sam, be careful," Mother would worry, "don't meet anybody on that bridge just up ahead." Bridges were narrow and treacherous, over all the little gullies and creeks. For two cars to try and cross them at the same time could be disastrous.

We rode on hot green summer afternoons, when the sun was paving the lake with diamonds or laying its lonely loveliness over the pastures and fields.

The gravel road pinged and crunched beneath the tires; the wind tore gloriously through as we sped along at the insane speed of thirty-five miles an hour.

We went riding in the cool of the evening, with sunset still lingering in the sky, and rode, just rode till the stars came out. This miracle of movement, to be carried by some force other than your own, how divine. And the fact that we were all together, Mother, Dad, the kids, and usually some nice old soul who otherwise never got out, added to its cozy consequence.

Almost immediately, even as today, our next passionate objective was to learn to drive. This happened with almost alarming ease. Drivers' licenses had not yet been invented. Anyone tall enough to reach the pedals and the steering wheel at the same time could. You learned by watching your father; or grimly, guttily, he taught you—and the battle royal was on as to who got the car even before it had cooled off at the curb and your weary parent trudged up the walk. Once this happened, you

didn't want to ride with your folks, you wanted to "joyride," which meant gathering a load of your peers and heading for a dance, a skating rink, or wickedly, a Sunday night movie, forbidden in Storm Lake, but available in some distant village of iniquity. Or—you just rode. And parked.

Ministers inveighed against joyriding as they did against dancing and cards. And a true inspiration of the devil it sometimes seemed to be. Especially in winter. Cars, once put up on blocks at the first snowfall, were now able to negotiate most main roads. Providing you first thawed them out with kettles of boiling water and didn't break an arm getting them to start. (Self-starters couldn't be depended on; every car still jutted its ornery but essential crank.) Then there was the trial of keeping icy side curtains buttoned down. Fiendish winds tore through the cracks in the isinglass. The wintry sins of joyriding were overrated—heaterless, bundled three feet deep in boots, blankets, mittens, ear muffs, and scarves—they were simply too hard to achieve!

Also, winter or summer, tires were always blowing out and your date had to jack up the car, wrench off the tire, examine the limp, ailing inner tube, scrape it, and then whack out a bright rubber patch to glue over its punctured flesh. Then he got out the pump and vigorously gave it artificial respiration. When it no longer wheezed, it was squeezed prayerfully back into the tire and the tire put back on the rim. Meanwhile, you froze by slow graceful inches in the car; or you got a quick deep freeze—and the reputation of being a good sport—by crawling painfully out and helping.

Blowouts were even more frequent in summer. The fierce Iowa heat and the blazing gravel were more than the strained, oft-patched lungs could endure—bang! They'd simply explode. Throughout the rescue operations you sweltered, sweat, and gasped sweet nothings at each other through clouds of dust kicked up by luckier vehicles. . . .

Coupes and sedans were replacing touring cars. Henry Ford had astounded and shocked the world by abandoning Lizzie. Yes, Lizzie—cheap, faithful, fruitful Lizzie, who had borne him so many customers so long. He was replacing her with some young hussy to be called a Model A—and it seemed a kind of betrayal. Great secrecy prevailed. No pictures were released. And at the local Ford agency all windows were draped until the proper day. Whether in mourning or for wedding veils was hard to say. Then you met the bride—and grinned, in a kind of reluctant relief. She was beautiful, most people agreed, "but still a Ford." Which meant something sturdy and economical and comfortably middle class. In short, American.

Many women were driving by then, and practically all their offspring, but few families boasted more than one car. There were no parking problems around our high school. Only the consolidated schools had school buses. We cosmopolitan town kids walked—even home for lunch, no matter how far we lived. After school we either walked in big, noisy bunches, or we bummed rides with the country kids who had to drive to get there. Or we swarmed over those other rare favorites of the gods who actually owned or had daily access to a car. Any parent rich or doting enough to provide it could convey instant popularity; overnight the plainest child could become a veritable Valentino or the school queen.

This will always be true to some degree. But it was infinitely more so then than today when a car is regarded not only as a status symbol, but practically a civil right!

With college, of course, the mysteries of distance vanished, the boundaries melted. We married and joined a mobile society, where parents spend half their waking hours on wheels; where children learn to dance and swim and ski, but don't learn to walk. "Going for a ride" cannot possibly hold the thrill for our youngsters that it had for us. Yet there is still something warm and wonderful about the family's piling into the car and setting off—for the supermarket, a drive-in movie, or a long vacation trip (despite the murder and mayhem that often occur in the back seat). Dad or Mother or a tall son driving. Young friends along, or some nice neighbor who otherwise might not get out for a ride.

The cars are big glass and steel splendors now, the highways broad and smooth, the hazards less from breakdowns and flat tires than traffic and speed. Yet something old-fashioned and eternal and curiously American remains. The sheer pleasure of locomotion—to view the world through moving windows . . . that new housing development, that bend in the road, that mountain, that lake . . . and do it with those you love.

FAREWELL, MY LOVELY!

E. B. White

I see by the new Sears Roebuck catalogue that it is still possible to buy an axle for a 1909 Model T Ford, but I am not deceived. The great days have faded, the end is in sight. Only one page in the current catalogue is devoted to parts and accessories for the Model T; yet everyone remembers springtimes when the Ford gadget section was larger than men's clothing, almost as large as household furnishings. The last Model T was built in 1927, and the car is fading from what scholars call the American scene — which is an understatement, because to a few million people who grew up with it, the old Ford practically *was* the American scene.

It was the miracle God had wrought. And it was patently the sort of thing that could only happen once. Mechanically uncanny, it was like nothing that had ever come to the world before. Flourishing industries rose and fell with it. As a vehicle, it was hard-working,

> *My own generation identifies it with Youth, with its gaudy, irretrievable excitements.*

commonplace, heroic; and it often seemed to transmit those qualities to the persons who rode in it. My own generation identifies it with Youth, with its gaudy, irretrievable excitements; before it fades into the mist, I would like to pay it the tribute of the sigh that is not a sob, and set down random entries in a shape somewhat less cumbersome than a Sears Roebuck catalogue.

There was this about a Model T: the purchaser never regarded his purchase as a complete, finished product. When you bought a Ford, you figured you had a start — a vibrant, spirited framework to which could be screwed an almost limitless assortment of decorative and functional hardware. Driving away from the agency, hugging the new wheel between your knees, you were already full of creative worry. . . .

First you bought a Ruby Safety Reflector for the rear, so that your posterior would glow in another's car's brilliance. Then you invested thirty-nine cents in some radiator Moto Wings, a popular ornament which gave the Pegasus touch to the machine and did something godlike to the owner. For nine cents you bought a fanbelt guide to keep the belt from slipping off the pulley.

You bought a radiator compound to stop leaks. This was as much a part of everybody's equipment as aspirin tablets are of a medicine cabinet. You bought special oil to prevent chattering, a clamp-on dash light, a patching outfit, a tool box which you bolted to the running board, a sun visor, a steering-column brace to keep the column rigid, and a set of emergency containers for gas, oil, and water . . . red for gas, gray for water, green for oil. It was only a beginning. After the car was about a year old, steps were taken to check the alarming disintegration. (Model T was full of tumors, but they were benign.) A set of anti-rattlers (ninety-eight cents) was a popular panacea. You hooked them on to the gas and spark rods, to the brake pull rod, and to the steering-rod connections. Hood silencers, of black rubber, were applied to the fluttering hood. Shock-absorbers and snubbers gave "complete relaxation." Some people bought rubber pedal pads, to fit over the standard metal pedals. (I didn't like these, I remember.) Persons of a suspicious or pugnacious turn of mind bought a rearview mirror; but most Model T owners weren't worried by what was coming from behind because they would soon enough see it out in front. They rode in a state of cheerful catalepsy.

Springtime in the heyday of the Model T was a delirious season. Owning a car was still a major excitement, roads were still wonderful and bad. The Fords were obviously conceived in madness: any car which was capable of going from forward into reverse without any perceptible mechanical hiatus was bound to be a mighty challenging thing to the human imagination. Boys used to veer them off the highway into a level pasture and run wild with them, as though they were cutting up with a girl. Most everybody used the reverse pedal quite as much as the regular foot brake—it distributed the wear over the bands and wore them all down evenly. That was the big trick, to wear all the bands down evenly, so that the final chattering would be total and the whole unit scream for renewal.

The days were golden, the nights were dim and strange. I still recall with trembling those loud, nocturnal crises when you drew up to a signpost and raced the engine so the lights would be bright enough to read destinations by. I have never been really planetary since. I suppose it's time to say good-bye. Farewell, my lovely!"

A family enjoys a holiday at the beach in their Model T Ford.

ROUTE 66

Called the Mother Road by John Steinbeck and the Glory Road by the Oakies fleeing the dust bowl, Route 66 became a large version of Main Street to most of America. Opened in 1926, it ran from Chicago to Los Angeles, stopping by such cities as St. Louis, Oklahoma City, Amarillo, Albuquerque, and Flagstaff. Route 66 was the first major road to connect states and allow easy travel across the country, and until the 1960s, it remained the ultimate road through the American frontier. It was a road of dreams, linking Americans through an endless string of billboards, diners, and motor courts.

Route 66's 2,400 miles stretched across three time zones. Although part of the highway was paved in 1926, much of it was just dirt and gravel. Driving was still a dirty, high-risk venture not for the faint at heart.

During the heyday of Route 66, motor courts were the accommodation of choice. The motels were often nothing more than a clean room with a wash basin and ranged in style from tepee-looking structures to individual, tile-roofed cottages. Choosing from the variety of motor courts that appeared along the highway's edge, travelers could usually easily find a vacancy, for reservations were not required, or accepted.

Would-be restaurant owners took advantage of the traffic along the highways and opened hundreds of diners boasting each day's blue plate special. The diners were gaudy, sometimes fanciful, structures and were filled with uniformed waitresses carrying the ubiquitous pot of coffee in one hand and a plate lunch and homemade pie in the other.

Before legislation outlawed billboard advertising too near the highway, Route 66 sported a roadside menagerie of colorful ads selling everything from cars to toiletries. In the days before television, the billboards kept travelers in touch with the latest products for sale and often offered entertainment as well. Burma Shave was one of the most legendary billboard advertisers, with such humorous slogans as "If your peach keeps out of reach, better practice what we preach—Burma Shave."

TIME OUT FOR HAPPINESS

Frank B. Gilbreth, Jr.

ll of the family but Grandma, who said that if necessary she'd rather crawl on her hands and knees, drove from Providence to Montclair in our gray Pierce Arrow touring car. Grandma, Tom Grieves, and Mrs. Cunningham all arrived separately by train.

Dad had named the Pierce Arrow "Foolish Carriage," because he said it was foolish for a man with a family as large as his to think he could afford such a fancy carriage. Mother, who was expecting another baby, sometimes must have thought that "Miss" would be a better first name than "Foolish," because Dad was both the world's worst and the world's most adventurous driver.

The car was equipped with a compact, homemade ice chest for baby bottles, and also with a specially tapered board which joined the folding swivel-seats in the back. The ice chest sat up front on the floor, near Mother's feet, and both it and the board provided extra seats for children.

Before we started on trips, we usually had speed drills to see whether we still had all our moxie when it came to putting up the isinglass side-curtains or changing a tire. We'd all be in the car, parked out front, and Dad would say, "All right, kids. Let's go with the curtains!" Then he'd press a stopwatch as we'd bail out, remove the front and back seats under which the curtains were stored, unfold the curtains themselves, snap them in place, with each child allocated specific ends of specific curtains, and put the seats back in.

The tire-changing drill was much the same, with the younger children hunting rocks to keep the car from rolling, and the older ones getting the spare tire from its case on the side of the car and rigging the jack. Meanwhile, Dad would strip off his coat and prepare to do the heavy work of operating the jack itself.

We never had any first-aid drills, because Dad was a supremely confident driver. But some of us thought such drills would be even more appropriate than the other ones.

Dad actually sought hairpin curves and potholes to test the car's mettle and hear the tires whine. He thought the best highway defense was a dashing offense. He believed that using the brakes, except as a last resort to cheat the Grim Reaper, denoted a craven lack of spirit. He enjoyed the symphony of blowing the Klaxon, tooting the bulb horn, grinding the gears, racing the engine, and shouting "roadhog!" He equated a car with pleasure, a tour with a joy ride, and speed with gaiety, and he liked to pull the hand throttle wide open, and then sit back and let her rip, while grinning in satisfaction or singing a silly raucous song.

We were all scared to ride with him; and Mother, who was scared to ride with *anybody*, was absolutely terrified. And on top of everything else, she knew there was always the possibility of his having a heart attack.

She'd clutch the newest and usually carsick baby—the Latest Model—to her bosom, hunching her arms, head, and shoulders around and over the child for protection. Meanwhile, she'd mutter over and over again, "Not so fast, Frank; not so fast."

And he'd open the windshield a little wider, for fuller enjoyment of the breeze, which immediately mounted from full gale to hurricane velocity, and reply in hurt tones: "Good Lord, Boss, we're hardly moving! You don't want me to get pinched for delaying traffic, do you?"

Despite Dad's bursts of speed, we never covered much territory in a day because the younger children required so many bathroom stops. For delicacy, these were referred to as "visiting Mrs. Murphy," and sometimes Mrs. Murphy had company twice an hour.

The boys would go on one side of the road, the girls on the other. And since we were all quite modest, we trudged pretty far back into the woods. The result was that it took a little over two days—with night stops in hotels at New Haven and Newark—to drive down the old Boston Post Road to Montclair.

But when we finally tooled up to the house

Dad had bought at 68 Eagle Rock Way, the whole trip . . . seemed worthwhile.

Lillie wrote of the family's arrival in Montclair: "Seen as they first saw it, in the fall, with the leaves gorgeous red and yellow . . . it

The 1907 painting The Turnpike *by George Dubuis depicts a weekend drive of yesteryear.*

seemed a fulfillment of a vision of the happy land. Dad had been careful not to describe the new home in detail. To keep their curiosity aroused and stimulate their excitement he stopped in front of many an old homestead and asked, 'Well, how do you like this?' . . . When he finally drove up to the place that was to be home, they could only tumble out, almost breathless with the thrill, and start to investigate the house, the garage, the hothouses, and all the possibilities of baseball fields, gardens, and homes for future pets."

Part of the tumbling out, of course, was abandoning ship, with the comforting realization that you had arrived alive and unmaimed.

Casey Jones

T. LAWRENCE SEIBERT

EDDIE NEWTON

1. Come all you round-ers if you want to hear a
2. Put in your wa-ter and shovel in your coal, put your
3. Ca - sey pulled up that Re - no hill, he

sto - ry a-bout a brave En - gi - neer;
head out the win - dow, watch them driv - ers roll; I'll
toot - ed for the cross-ing with an aw - ful shrill; The

Cas - ey Jones was the Round - er's name On a
run her till she leaves the rail, 'Cause I'm
switch - men knew by the en - gine's moan, That the

six eight wheel - er boys he won his fame. The
eight hours late with the west - ern mail. He
man at the throt - tle was Ca - sey Jones. He

call - er called Ca - sey at a half past four,
looked at his watch and his watch was slow, He
pulled up with - in two miles of the place,

"Put your head out the window, watch those drivers roll...."

Kissed his wife at the station door, he
looked at the wa-ter and the wa-ter was low, he
Num-ber four stared him right in the face; he

mount-ed to the Cab-in with his or-ders in hand, and he took his fare-well trip to the
turned to the Fire - man and he said, we're go-ing to reach Fris-co but we'll
turned to the Fire - man, "Boy, bet-ter jump, cause there's two lo-co-mo-tives that's a

Prom - ised Land. Ca-sey Jones! mount-ed to the ca-bin, Oh
all be dead. Ca-sey Jones! go-ing to reach Fris-co, Oh
go-ing to bump. Ca-sey Jones! two lo-co-mo-tives, Oh

Ca-sey Jones! with his or-ders in his hand; Ca-sey Jones!
Ca-sey Jones! but we'll all be dead; Ca-sey Jones!
Ca-sey Jones! that's a go-ing to bump; Ca-sey Jones!

mount-ed to the ca-bin, and he took his fare-well trip to the Prom-ised Land.
go-ing to reach Fris-co, we're go-ing to reach Fris-co but we'll all be dead.
two lo-co-mo-tives, there's two lo-co-mo-tives that's a go-ing to bump.

THE RAILROAD

E. B. White

*W*hat's the railroad to me? / I never go to see / Where it ends. / It fills a few hollows, / And makes banks for the swallows, / It sets the sand a-blowing, / And the blackberries a-growing."

Henry Thoreau, who wrote those lines, was a student of railroading. He was a devotee, though seldom a passenger. He lived, of course, in the morningtime of America's railroads. He was less concerned with where the railroad ended than with what the railroad meant, and his remarks on the Fitchburg seem fadeproof in the strong light of this century, their liturgical quality still intact.

And what's the railroad to me? I have to admit that it means a great deal to me. It fills more than a few hollows. It is the link with my past, for one thing, and with the city, for another—two connections I would not like to see broken.

Bangor is the second-oldest railroad town in New England; a steam train pulled out of Bangor, bound upriver for Old Town, on November 6, 1836. The running time for the twelve-mile trip was two and a half hours, the conductor's name was Sawyer, passengers were aboard, and the fare was thirty-seven and a half cents. That was the first steam train to roll in Maine, the second to roll in New England. Soon Bangor may set another mark in rail history; it may watch the departure of the last train, and as this sad hulk moves off down the track (if it ever does), Maine will become the first state in the Union, except for Hawaii, to have no rail passenger service between its major cities. . . .

I made my first rail journey into Maine in the summer of 1905, and have been riding to and fro on the cars ever since. On that first trip, when I was led by the hand into the green sanctuary of a Pullman drawing room and saw spread out for my pleasure its undreamed-of facilities and its opulence and the porter holding the pillow in his mouth while he drew the clean white pillowcase up around it and the ladder to the upper and the three-speed electric fan awaiting my caprice at the control switch and the little hammock slung so cunningly to receive my clothes and the adjoining splendor of the toilet room with its silvery appointments and gushing privacy, I was fairly bowled over with childish admiration and glee, and I fell in love with railroading then and there and have not been the same boy since that night.

We were a family of eight, and I was the youngest member. My father was a

A steam train races down the track toward its next destination.

thrifty man, and come the first of August every summer, he felt that he was in a position to take his large family on a month's vacation. His design, conceived in 1905 and carried out joyously for many summers, was a simple one: for a small sum he rented a rough camp on one of the Belgrade lakes, then turned over the rest of his savings to the railroad and the Pullman Company in return for eight first-class round-trip tickets and plenty of space on the sleeper—

a magnificent sum, a magnificent gesture. When it came to travel, there was not a second-class bone in my father's body, and although he spent thousands of hours of his life sitting bolt upright in dusty day coaches, commuting between Mount Vernon and Grand Central, once a year he put all dusty things aside and lay down, with his entire family, in Pullman perfection, his wife fully dressed against the possibility of derailment, to awake next morning in the winy air of a spruce-clad land and to debouch, surrounded by his eager children and full of the solemnity of trunk checks, onto the platform of the Belgrade depot, just across the tracks from Messalonskee's wild, alluring swamp. As the express train pulled

The conductor greets his passengers with a smile.

away from us in Belgrade on that August morning of 1905, I got my first glimpse of this benign bog, which did not seem dismal to me at all. It was an inseparable part of the first intoxication of railroading, and, of all natural habitats, a swamp has ever since been to me the most beautiful and most seductive. . . .

When I came to live in Maine, the depot was twenty-three miles away, in Ellsworth. Then the depot got to be fifty miles away, in Bangor. After tomorrow night, it will be a hundred and forty miles away (for a sleeping car), in Portland. A year from now, there may be no depot in the whole state—none with a light burning, that is. I cannot conceive of my world without a rail connection, and perhaps I shall have to pull up stakes and move to some busier part of the swamp, where the rails have not been abandoned. Whether I move away or stay put, if the trains of Maine come to a standstill I will miss them greatly. I will miss cracking the shade at dawn . . . and the breakfast in bed, drinking from the punctured can of grapefruit juice as we proceed gravely up the river, and the solid old houses of Gardiner, and Augusta's little trackslide glade with the wooden staircase and the vines of the embankment and the cedar waxwing tippling on berries as I tipple on juice. I'll miss the peaceful stretches of the river above Augusta, with the stranded sticks of pulpwood along the banks; the fall overcast, the winter brightness; the tiny blockhouse of Fort Halifax, at Winslow, mighty bastion of defense; and at Waterville the shiny black flanks of Old No. 470, the Iron Horse that has been enshrined right next to what used to be the Colby campus. . . .

Early last spring, as my train waited on a

siding for another train to go through, I looked out of the window and saw our conductor walking in the ditch, a pocketknife in his hand. He passed out of sight and was gone ten minutes, then reappeared. In his arms was a fine bunch of pussy willows, a gift for his wife, I don't doubt. It was a pleasing sight, a common episode, but I recall feeling at the time that the scene was being overplayed, and that it belonged to another century. The railroads will have to get on with the action if they are to boost that running speed from twenty-eight to forty and lure customers.

Perhaps the trains will disappear from Maine forever, and the conductor will then have the rest of his life to cut pussies along the right of way, with the sand a-blowing and the blackberries a-growing. I hope it doesn't happen in my lifetime, for I think one well-conducted institution may still regulate a whole country.

[Two years later.] In those last days of the rails in Maine, I remember most clearly the remark of a Bangor citizen, which I read in the paper. This fellow walked downtown on the day after the razing of the depot; he stared in surprise at the new vista. "Hey!" he said. "You can see Brewer from Exchange Street!" (Brewer is Bangor's twin, a few hundred yards distant across the river.)

In the old days, when the railroads were in their prime, you couldn't see Brewer from Exchange Street, but you could close your eyes and see the continent of America stretched out in front of you, with the rails running on endlessly into the purple sunset, as in an overwritten novel. I loved it when I couldn't see Brewer from Exchange Street, the rest of the view was so good.

The Train

I love to watch it on the track
Negotiate a curve,
I love to hear it whistle back
and blow its breath in swirls,
And hear it puffing at a grade
And then go racing down,
When through a cut the rhythm fades
Then hurry toward the town.

It fills its flanks at waiting tanks
And masticates the coal,
Manipulates between the banks
And then like thunder rolls,
It wriggles through the tunnel then
Before the crossing screams,
It scurries round a meadow bend
And waves its hat of steam.

Then stately moves across the bridge
The bell its message toll,
And just beyond that low flung ridge
To circumvent a knoll.
It draws a string of freighted cars
The hills and valleys gulp,
Then chugs into the railroad yards
And then its racing stops.

Oh, trains of steam and engineers
When once you rode the rails,
When children from their windows peered
And listened for the bells,
The bell is silent as the men
Who blew the whistle's blast,
In memory hear them race again
And by my cottage pass.

Helen Monnette

A BROWN-STOCKING EASTER

Jo Cudd

*I*n the mid-1930s, when I was about five years old, my family lived in the tiny town of Guion, Arkansas, in the foothills of the Ozark Mountains. My father worked for the Missouri Pacific Railroad, whose tracks, in our part of the state, ran adjacent to the White River. Like most other families of that era who had been greatly affected by the depression years, we did not own a car. What traveling we did, which was not much, was always by rail. Young and curious, I was thrilled by any kind of outing; so I was doubly excited about a prospective Easter Day trip to visit cousins who lived fifty miles north of us in the small village of Old Joe. They did not live directly on the railroad but were within reasonable walking distance of the nearest depot at Berry. My family planned to take a picnic lunch and Easter eggs and catch the early train north to Berry, where our relatives would meet us. We would all have several hours to enjoy an egg hunt and picnic before catching the southbound train for home.

On Easter Eve, as my family colored eggs and prepared food for the next day's lunch, my excitement and anticipation almost equaled that of Christmas. I was the first one awake on Easter morning. As I lay by my sleeping sister, eyed my new dress hanging on the back of a chair, and thought contentedly about the day ahead, it slowly dawned on me that it was too quiet outside. I heard no birds singing or movement of any kind, and I began to suspect that the almost too bright light creeping in from outside was not just the pre-sunrise daylight. What ordinarily would have filled me with joy caused my heart to sink as I raised the shade to find everything covered with a mantle of white.

My dad, even under the best of circumstances, was not the most enthusiastic traveler in the state. Ordinarily, it took no more than a heavy frost to give him an excuse for backing out of a trip, so my hopes were close to nil as my sister and I trailed disconsolately into the kitchen for breakfast. Our faces must have expressed our dashed anticipation because my dad looked at us and didn't do much hemming and hawing before saying he "guessed we would just go along for the ride anyway but not to be surprised if no one met us at the train station."

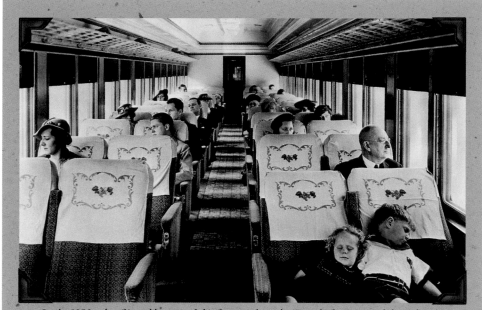

In the 1930s, the adjustable seats of this day coach on the "Royal Blue" train of the Baltimore and Ohio Railroad line left ample room for catching up on one's sleep.

We did, of course, have to forfeit our Easter dresses and had to dig out and wear the long brown stockings that I hated and thought I'd seen the last of until the next winter; but my excitement was unbounded as we boarded the train and headed north. As we reached Berry, the sun emerged from the clouds and there stood our cousins with "wait and see" looks upon their faces, wondering if we were possibly on that train. The whole world was white and sparkly, and after the train pulled away, it was as if we were lost in a winter wonderland, with no one else for miles around. We spread our picnic on the porch of the depot and my cousins hunted eggs in the snow, never knowing if the tracks we followed would lead to a "find" or if they were merely a false trail left by our parents. The day was filled with smiles, and my "brown-stocking Easter" has since become one of my dearest childhood memories.

As we rush, as we rush in the train,
The trees and the houses go wheeling back,
But the starry heavens above that plain
Come flying on our track.

James Thomson

THE FAMILY VACATION

For decades, summers have meant time for the annual family vacation. Dressed in their traveling finery, everyone would board the nearest train or load the family car and anticipate a long stay at the beach or visiting relatives. At first, roadside amenities and exciting final destinations were limited, but the family vacation would soon change. The newly established national parks gave American families a favorite destination (such as the Glacier Hotel pictured at left), the new road systems provided an easy means of travel, and the Kodak camera made preserving all the trip's memories easier than ever.

"OLD FAITHFUL" GEYSER, YELLOWSTONE NATIONAL PARK—18

In 1872, Wyoming's Yellowstone National Park became the first national park in the world, based mostly on its geological phenomena: hot springs, fossil forests, and geysers (including Old Faithful, pictured at right). In the decades to follow, thanks to the efforts of such early environmentalists as John Muir, national parks were established nationwide and vacationing Americans could easily enjoy the country's national jewels.

Before 1912, Americans found traveling the country's rough dirt roads an adventure. By the time the country had a million car owners, they were ready to trade in adventure for comfort. The Lincoln Highway Association was started to raise money for a central highway system, and with the help of the federal government, smooth paved roads became more than a dreamer's vision.

In the early 1900's, middle class Americans began taking their home-built campers, revamped automobiles, and self-made "recreational vehicles" south for the winter. These travellers became known as the "tin can tourists." While some "tin cans" were quite elegant and outfitted with such features as stained-glass windows, most were contraptions with everything a camper would need strapped to the roof.

High-school dropout George Eastman first made photography accessible to the average American in 1888 with his $25 black box camera. The small, new camera had only three simple steps: pull a string to cock the shutter, turn a key to advance the film, and press the trigger. When the customer's 100-exposure roll of film was used up, he sent it back to Eastman for developing and reloading.

George Eastman named his new camera and film company Kodak, and his motto became, "You press the button, we do the rest." His cameras kept getting simpler; and in the early part of the century, children around the nation were saving for the one-dollar price of a Kodak Brownie camera.

When automobiles were first invented, road maps did not exist and most routes were unmarked. It wasn't until 1901 that automobile associations began making travel guides, such as the Blue Book, which mapped specific routes. Maps replaced travel guides in the 1920s after states gave their roads official numbers. Before then, one road could have several names, depending on which direction you were heading.

ESPECIALLY FATHER

Gladys Taber

*W*hy don't we take a trip to northern Michigan?" [Father] said. "It is fine country up there."

"It's better right here," said Mamma. "Why don't you take a day off and read the *National Geographic*?"

Mamma felt she had taken trips enough with him before the cottage was built. We had gone constantly, and Mamma and I simply dreaded those little trips. Maybe we would have enjoyed them if we could have gone comfortably and really seen the great country.

But Father wanted to rough it, and rough it we did. Gadgets for motoring were not yet on the market, hotel accommodations were scarce and not always good, the day of the motel was far off. Roads were poorly marked or not marked at all. Most of them were detours.

But Father had fixed everything. He built two long black boxes the size of coffins and looking just like coffins, which he screwed to the running boards of the big old Keeton he was driving. When they were in place, the only way to get in the car was to climb up and leap like a gazelle. One side of the car was sealed off permanently as that box was built up to the window. The boxes were made of the heaviest lumber, the biggest screws, the longest spikes, for Father liked things strong. They were padlocked with great locks; one of his phobias was that someone would steal something if he turned his back a minute.

On the car top went suitcases and more boxes, roped and lashed to withstand a hurricane. We never had hurricanes in Wisconsin, but one never could tell. Inside the car were layers and layers of bedding, pillows, raincoats, sweaters, knapsacks. This was topped with Father's shovel, his mining engineer's pick, camera equipment, and above all, up under the roof, the large Irish setter, Timmie, and me.

The tent was lashed on in back, and the tent pole ran the length of the car over everything else. Yards and yards of black mosquito netting fitted in around Mamma.

Pots and pans and kitchen utensils and canned goods filled the coffins. Father never expected to be able to buy anything after we left the home town. He was a frustrated explorer, equipped for either a safari or an Arctic trip whenever we traveled.

We always left around five in the morning for "We better make a good early start," Father

We must have been poorer than usual, but my world was furnished richly with the gifts of the sea.

would say, "or we'll never get anywhere."

By the time the car was loaded, the house closed, Mamma, Timmie and I settled, we were worn out. Mamma wore her long duster, goggles and a thick veil. Father wore his mining clothes, which gave him a rakish air. They were too heavy for these motor trips so after the first ten miles, he began to pull things off. I wore a middy suit, a duster, and a sailor hat. . . .

I remember the places. In California, Father set up his little family in a tent in Tent City. We went swimming every day. I floated in the salt greenish water beside him, keeping up by clinging with one hand to his shoulder. I was too young to swim, but I could go anywhere with Father doing the breast stroke powerfully beside me.

We bought oranges in washtubs at twenty-five cents a tub. This impressed me because Father and Mamma kept marveling at it. The New England Christmas orange was a long way from this.

Cooking was sketchy. We bought food at a delicatessen, and I thought store potato salad in a cardboard box was simply wonderful.

But the best was walking the beach with Father. Every shell was a mystery and a story. The seaweed was a book in itself, as Father talked about it. I gathered the long cool rubbery strands, filled my pockets with sand dollars and small pale shells and struggled after

Father's rapid steps. It's possible he was out of a job, for we must have been poorer than usual, but my world was furnished richly with the gifts of the sea. . . .

The stars overhead had their romance, too. Everything visible to man's eye was a marvel. The great tides moved by the moon excited Father, so did the track of a small greenish snail on wet sand. . . .

When we packed up to move that time, I kept a small

A young brother and sister enjoy the treasures of their vacation at the beach.

candy box of sea treasures, the pearl-lined, the silver, the pinkish. The wafer-like sand dollar was there, and the starfish, and Father let me keep a small bit of kelp too.

A BUS OF MY OWN

Jim Lehrer

I loved working in the bus depot. I loved being the guy who breathed into the PA microphone and then cried out to the world: "May I have your attention, please! This is your first call for the Continental Trailways 5:15 P.M. Air-Conditioned Silversides Thruliner to Houston and Dallas, now leaving from lane one next to the building for: Inez, Edna, Ganado, Louise, El Campo, Pierce, Wharton, Hungerford, Kendleton, Beasley, Rosenberg, Richmond, Sugarland, Stafford, Missouri City and Houston. Connecting in Houston for Huntsville, Buffalo, Corsicana, Dallas, Fort Worth, Wichita Falls, Amarillo, Tucumcari, Albuquerque, Flagstaff, Los Angeles, San Diego, San Francisco, Portland and Seattle. Connecting in Dallas for Tyler, Longview, Shreveport, Minden, Natchez, Jackson, Meridian, Montgomery, Columbus, Fayetteville, Raleigh, Richmond, Washington, New York City and Boston . . . and for Ardmore, Oklahoma City, Wichita, Topeka, Kansas City, Des Moines and Minneapolis . . . Jefferson City, Columbia, St. Louis, Indianapolis, Columbus and Pittsburgh . . . Hannibal, Quincy, Peoria, Chicago, Benton Harbor, Kalamazoo and Detroit. Connecting in Houston also for Baytown, Goose Creek, Dayton, Liberty, Beaumont, Port Arthur,

Pensacola, Tallahassee, Tampa and Miami. All aboard, please! Don't forget your baggage, please!

Orange, Lake Charles, Kinder, Opelousas, Lafayette, Baton Rouge, New Orleans, Gulfport, Biloxi, Mobile, Pensacola, Tallahassee, Tampa and Miami . . . All aboard, please! Don't forget your baggage, please!"

It is only good reporting to say my bus-calling became quite famous in and around the Victoria bus station. People didn't exactly come from miles around to hear me call the 5:15, but it was almost that bad—or good. When I first went to work, I read the names from a loose-leaf notebook. But after a while I had them memorized. And I could go through the entire call without looking down. And it was not only the Houston-Dallas route. I also had in my head and on my tongue the call southwest to Inairi, Vidairi, Refugio (pronounced re-*frur*-ee-oh), Woodsboro, Sinton, Odem, Calallen and Corpus Christi. Connecting to Robstown, Alice, Freer and Laredo . . . and to Kingsville, Falfurrias,

A New York bus line awaits its next passengers.

Hometown Lights

How wonderful to see the lights
Of your hometown spring into view!
You've come so far, the miles were long,
But now your journey's through.
"Oh, welcome, Wanderer, welcome home!"
The winking lights all seem to say,
And streets hold out their arms to you
As if to bid you stay.

So many dear, familiar things
Are still a part of you,
That suddenly your heart leaps up
With joy that you once knew.
Loved ones to greet, old friends to meet,
Reliving times of long ago.
Ah, 'tis a magic time indeed;
The sweetest one can know.

And somehow, precious times like these
Can never, ever quite depart;
The traveler stores them all away
And keeps them in his heart.
And when in distant climes he fares,
Wherever he may roam,
Within his sweetest dreams he'll see
The twinkling lights of home.

Thelma E. Foster

Raymondville, Edinburg, McAllen, Harlingen, Brownsville and points in Old Mexico. There was also one northwest to San Antonio through Nursery, Thomaston, Cuero, Westhoff, Smiley, Nixon, Pandora, Stockdale, Sutherland Springs and Sayers Crossroads, plus one north to Austin through Yoakum, Shiner, Gonzales, Luling and Lockhard, and another straight south through Bloomington and Plaedo to Port Lavaca and the waters of the Gulf of Mexico.

Some of the drivers, particularly a delightful man named Paul Guthrie, used to walk up and stare right at me in mock stunned rapture as I called out the towns one after another in my phony, syrupy, pretentious, Texasy nineteen-year-old PA voice. Paul said I should put out a record titled *Famous Bus Calls I Have Made* by Jimmy Charles Leher.

Family, Friends, and the Front-Porch Swing:
MEMORIES OF HOME

I Remember, I Remember

I remember, I remember,
The house where I was born,
The little window where the sun
Came peeping in at morn:
He never came a wink too soon,
Nor brought too long a day;
But now, I often wish the night
Had borne my breath away.

I remember, I remember,
The roses, red and white;
The violets, and the lily-cups,
Those flowers made of light!
The lilacs where the robin built,
And where my brother set
The laburnum on his birthday—
The tree is living yet!

I remember, I remember,
The fir trees dark and high;
I used to think their slender tops
Were close against the sky:
It was a childish ignorance,
But now 'tis little joy
To know I'm farther off from heaven
Than when I was a boy.

Thomas Hood

The painting Homestead *by American artist George Oberteuffer depicts a peaceful day at home.*

TO REMEMBER FOREVER

Gladys Hasty Carroll

I went home every weekend, and the weekends were heavenly. Every Saturday I hurried up Central Avenue to the open electric in the Upper Square. . . . Sometimes Harold rode with me; but if he did, when we got off in the village he went down Main Street to the Dr. Sanborn house and I went up Portland Street to my father's paintshop for the ride home behind Pony, the big white workhorse who pulled all our workloads and was our only means of conveyance since first my grandfather's Old Belle and then her once fleetfooted daughter Bess had been turned out to pasture.

All the way along the sandy road, past Clara Warren's little house and big flower garden riotous in late June with huge Oriental poppies, David Hanson's milk farm, and Woodlawn Cemetery; through Old Swamps, across the railroad tracks of the Boston and Maine Eastern Division, over Agamenticus Bridge, on to Ed Goodwin's hill; past Witchtrot Road, Nason's pump, the district schoolhouse; down Nason's hill, through the woods, over White's Marsh Bridge; past Dorr's Gate, the Boston place, the old Min Joy place, we talked. I told him where I had been and what I had done; he told me what had happened while I was away—how far along the haying was, what vegetables were at their prime, who had come to spend the day. By the time we turned up the lane and into the dooryard I was reoriented. It was as if I had been gone only for an hour or two, except that everything now stood out for me, every smallest thing three-dimensional, like a separate piece of sculpture; every sound, however soft or low, distinct from every other; and the smells—oh, the good, familiar smells. . . . It was in every way another world from that of the city, even of a small city.

It was as if I had been gone only for an hour or two. . . .

Remember running up the porch steps; seeing the dish towels on the line above the railing boxes full of house plants taking their summer outing; hugging and kissing my grandfather, who sat there in visored cap and a wool jacket over his gingham shirt, . . . feeling the softness of his gray side-whiskers and mustache; trying to give him part of whatever I had that he was growing short of.

"Well, Gladie," he always said. "Home again, be ye?"

Yes. Yes, I was home again.

Remember going through the small entry, seeing the high hooks and the low hooks (though there were no children now to use the low hooks), and on into the kitchen where my mother and Aunt Vinnie were sewing or mending, each by her own back window, unless one of them was starting the fire in the kitchen stove for supper or my mother had gone into the parlor to do for Grammy. Auntie had given up the parlor to Grammy when we came home in the spring and now slept in what had been Harold's chamber. Whenever I was here I slept with Grammy, so that I could give her the care she needed at night and my mother could have uninterrupted sleep. . . .

Remember all their faces— Mother's, Auntie's, Grammy's— and their dark percale dresses, their bright percale aprons. Though she could go only to her platform rocker by the window which looked out upon the lane, Grammy would never have left her bedside without an apron on.

Remember how clean the house was—a cleanliness impossible where there are many things, especially many rugs, cushions, and pieces of upholstered furniture. In the kitchen a dining table, six straight chairs, a dropleaf table with a tidy newspaper and the mending basket on it, a wooden couch padded with a folded quilt and covered with a flowered cretonne "throw"; a clock on the mantel; a scrubbed pine floor; on the wall a Currier and

Ives print, and a comb case under a small mirror. In the sitting room the sewing machine, the Windsor chairs, a willow rocker, a horsehair-covered couch which could be opened into a bed, the Larkin desk with two shelves of books, three small braided rugs on an oiled floor, and on the mantel over the small fireplace the luster

Many fond memories include Grandmother with her sewing basket.

pitcher, the blue glass basket, and perhaps a mug full of sweet peas. In my grandfather's room his four-poster with the corn-husk mattress and the dotted blue calico spread, his chest of drawers, and on his shelf the tall green bottle from which he drank night and morning a swallow of the herb tonic he made himself; nothing else; he will not have even a strip of straw matting on the floor. No curtains in any

A woman proudly poses before her Indianapolis home and her rose-covered porch in 1900.

of these rooms; only rolled green shades to pull down against strong sunlight if need be.

Nobody was ever surprised to see me. I was never surprised to be there. The surprising thing always was, and is, to become conscious that I am somewhere else—that I, the person who was here, am in another place.

The smell of those rooms, in summer, is always of the summer fields and woods which stretch out farther than the eye can see from all their open doors and windows. . . .

But the room at the end of the long front hall, which used to be the parlor and Auntie's room and now was Grammy's had its own smell. The parlor furniture was stored in the shed chamber, and she had by her (except for the piano) only what she used: her bed, her platform rocker, . . . her table piled with books and magazines, her windowsill lined with bottles of medicine, and two or three chairs for visitors. But the flowered, ingrain carpet was still on the floor. . . . The lace curtains, though too old for many more launderings, were still at the windows. . . . My proud little grandmother, now stooped to less than her own five feet in height and with one of her tiny, slim-fingered hands useless, reads avidly every mention of Queen Mary of England and greatly loves both princes. So it was age Grammy's room smelled of, for she never wanted a window open, said she had enough air from the door. Lady, bed quilts, carpets, curtains, books; all as clean as what is old can be. . . .

And home was waiting for me. That weekend was like all the other weekends of the summer, except that Sunday afternoon I did not have to leave when Harold did. I walked to the end of the lane with him. Goldenrod and wild blue asters were beginning to bloom among the sweetfern. It was coming back-to-school time, but I was not going back anywhere. I was heading out into a stiff breeze, and the cables, one by one, were being slipped.

Harold stopped and smiled down, put his hands on my shoulders.

"Well, good luck, little sister," he said. "Let me know if you need anything. I'll take care of the first term bill when it comes. You'll have a great time."

I nodded. We kissed. I watched him almost out of sight. He turned and waved I turned and walked in the opposite direction.

When I got home, my father had brought down the dome-covered wood-and-steel trunk from the shed chamber, and he and my mother were scrubbing it with brushes. I watched my father carry it, when it was clean, into the sit-

The smell of those rooms, in summer, is always of the summer fields and woods which stretch out farther than the eye can see from all their open doors and windows.

ting room. It stood there empty, with the cover raised, and all the next two days were adding to the heap around it. The great heap of things they thought I would need at college . . . A bed pillow, patchwork quilts, the Indian blanket my father had won by paying ten cents for a number which turned out to be the lucky one; the winter coat to keep me warm, the shoes and rubbers to keep my feet dry, the graduation dresses, the skirts and blouses, the sweaters, the bureau scarf, the toilet things, the fountain pen on the black ribbon which would hang around my neck so I would not lose it, the towels and facecloths, the family photographs, the underwear.

"It will *never* all go in the trunk!" I cried, despairing.

"In the trunk and your valise. I think it will," my mother told me. "When it's all together I'll show you how."

She showed me by doing it the night before I was to go, after everyone but us had gone to bed. She knelt and I passed her things carefully folded. She fitted them together like a jigsaw puzzle. . . . She smiled up at me as she knelt before the trunk which had gone with her to Rochester before I was born, and I smiled back; but we could not see each other very well. . . .

The next morning they called me early. I bathed at the big flowered china bowl and put on a suit my mother had made over from a suit once worn by a friend of hers who lived in

Pasadena, California. . . . Grammy lay watching me. I went along the hall carrying my valise, my pocketbook, my brown cotton gloves, and the brown velvet hat which had been Jennie's.

"I got the trunk locked," said my father, "and it's loaded into the wagon. Here's the key. Put it where you won't lose it."

I sat at the breakfast table. It was all a blur. Mother was not there. She had gone in to help Grammy.

"Better get started," my father said. "Trains don't wait."

I went into the parlor and kissed Grammy and my mother good-bye.

"Act like a lady," said Grammy, "wherever you go."

My mother did not say anything. She was crying. She held me as if she could not let me go.

I went out alone into the sitting room and put on my hat and gloves.

My grandfather was still at the kitchen table. He was staring into the distance. I kissed his cheek. Then he looked at me. I saw how old his eyes were.

"Well," he said. "Well—come home when you can."

"Where is Auntie?" I asked.

He shook his head.

The door was open into the shedroom. I went out there. She was building a fire in the stove. I don't know why. I doubt if she did. I stood watching her shake the oil over the wood from a bottle with a quill in the cork. She dropped in a match and replaced the cover.

"I suppose you're ready to set sail," she said.

There was a faint smell of kerosene and wood smoke in the air.

"Now don't cry," she said. "You wanted to go and you're going. Remember what you wrote in your class poem?"

I couldn't remember a word of it.

"The last verse," she said, and repeated it:

So for us the sun is rising
Sending forth red glowing rays.
Omens of a gleaming future,
Prophets of successful days.
And about us brightly smiling
Is the fairness of the morn,
For to us, all bravely ready,
'Tis not evening—but dawn.

"It's not a very good poem," I said.

"No," Auntie agreed. "Whatever else you may be going to be, I don't think you're going to be a poet. But the idea is good. Your sun *is* rising. You've got your day ahead of you. Now see what you can do with it."

She gave me a quick kiss and went around the stove to the woodbox.

"Let us hear from you," she said, stooping until I could not see her face.

"I'll—write every day," I promised. And fled.

Down the lane. Past the old Min Joy place, Boston's, Dorr's gate. Over White's Marsh Bridge, through the woods, up Nason's hill, past the schoolhouse, down Goodwin's hill, across the tracks of the Eastern Division of the Boston and Maine. Through Old Swamps, past Woodlawn Cemetery; then to Powder House Hill, my father's paintshop, down Portland Street into the village square, and along Main Street to the New Hampshire line and the Salmon Falls railroad station. . .

Away, away, away.

An attic trunk holds souvenirs of yesterday.

Upon Returning

Is this the lane where lilacs used to bloom —
Or have I missed the road that once I knew?
As here above the fence, no longer loom
The wind-blown lilacs I had longed to view.
For years I somehow knew I would come back —
Although a silent voice had said to me:
Old scenes will be subdued, in someway lack
The beauty known upon each hill and lea!

But yet, I know I will return again
To claim a dream before it fades and dies;
To see a greening hillside washed in rain
And soon, the clearness of the cobalt skies.
I will return again I know — I know —
To walk remembered paths of long ago.

May Smith White

WHAT BECAME OF AMERICA'S FRONT PORCHES?

Marcos Flecha

Wander in the old section of any city and you will see something you will never see in the newer ones: front porches. They have become something like the old hitching posts, the dying relics of another time. Like the end of an era, the front porch went out in the face of the automobile, air conditioning, television, the high-intensity streetlight, the commercialization of American leisure time.

How the front porch came to be added to the American home is a thing not easy to trace, although it is not at all difficult to understand that before air conditioning and other features of contemporary life, it must have held much fascination. Presumably, it was intended for people to catch the evening breeze. It was on the front porch that Americans of a past era cemented family ties, strengthened political and religious beliefs, and practiced a more moral life. Because it was public, it was a place where youngsters learned to say "Yes, sir" to Dad, where they learned to love and respect Grandmother's advanced age, and where the younger members of the family dropped what they had learned on the street.

On the front porch, conversation was always embarrassingly unsophisticated. What one saw from it was something almost pastoral: subtle, cool darkness, children skating, young couples strolling and—across the street—the neighbors watching the same thing.

From the porch at night we watched the fireflies, scanned the skies for a shooting star, and listened to children's classics.

Like the parlor before it, the front porch was one of the approved courting places—in many homes, the only one. Hearing a porch swing squeaking far into the night, one knew that the girl next door was being courted. And it was not at all unusual to pass a brightly lit and decorated porch on which a party was going on. There was little, if any, adult supervision of front porch courting or partying; it was taken for granted that the boy who came there, being on the family premises, would behave and respect the home, the family and the girl. And most of the time he did.

As the youngest of six brothers and sisters, I used to stand on the porch at three each day and watch as they came streaming back from the grown-up world of school. They would cross First Street, Second, Third, and then all begin a race toward the house, short-cutting through the lot over six private paths worn into the grass. . . .

Perhaps at that time there was nothing for adults to do or any place for them to go, but after it warmed up enough to loiter on the porch, that was where we spent most of our time. When the sun began to sink and we had eaten, Father would take up his favorite position on the porch, which was on the deck with his back against the house. Then Mother would come out with her chair to sit beside him. Gradually we tired of playing and began to gather around, starting those endless questions that ranged from where the grass went in winter to why there were stars in the sky. . . .

. . . There was no question we could ask that did not eventually lead back to God. Father would read the Bible to us for hours. He seemed never to be without it—always reading it, always deep in wonder over what it said.

Then there were the nights when uncles, aunts, and cousins would gather on the long porch to visit. The men at one end talked about things they liked to talk about; the women at the other end talked about their things; and the yard ran full of yelling children. . . .

. . . From the porch at night we watched the fireflies, scanned the skies for a shooting star and listened to children's classics that today's children have most likely never heard. On the front porch, we were insulated from outside influences, for there only we, our relatives, and our dearest friends gathered, and we were not yet old enough to wander beyond our yard.

In September and October the winds began to change. From the porch I could see the cornstalks change to a bright yellow, the grass slowly turn brown and Father's garden gradually disappear. The porch was not yet unbearably cold and from it each night we watched the slow rising of an incredibly large and yellow moon. And by now, as there were no children running and yelling, we began to detect a certain loneliness in the night.

Leaning against a post and looking out over the night, Father would patiently explain the meaning of the thickening loneliness. Human life was something like that too. It began with a weak green spring, then came a hot and playful summer, a quiet maturing autumn and then the winter. He was somewhere between summer and autumn and we, of course, were still in our weak green spring.

The front porch remained a factor in American family life until World War II, when disorder began to come to it. In the great upheaval of war, customs and morals began to change. The front porch seemingly went off to war and never made it back.

Are we ready for it again? We have flown the full circle and nowhere else can we go but back to the green leaf, the clear stream, the blue sky and to real communities . . . perhaps back to the front porch.

GROWING UP

Russell Baker

*M*orrisonville was a poor place to prepare for a struggle with the twentieth century, but a delightful place to spend a childhood. It was summer days drenched with sunlight, fields yellow with buttercups, and barn lofts sweet with hay. . . .

On a broiling afternoon when the men were away at work and all the women napped, I moved through majestic depths of silences, silences so immense I could hear the corn growing. Under these silences there was an orchestra of natural music playing notes no city child would ever hear. A certain cackle from the henhouse meant we had gained an egg. The creak of a porch swing told of a momentary breeze blowing across my grandmother's yard. Moving past Liz Virts's barn as quietly as an Indian, I could hear the swish of a horse's tail and knew the horseflies were out in strength. As I tiptoed along a mossy bank to surprise a frog, a faint splash told me the quarry had spotted me and slipped into the stream. Wandering among the sleeping houses, I learned that tin roofs crackle under the power of the sun, and when I tired and came back to my grandmother's house, I padded into her dark cool living room, lay flat on the floor, and listened to the hypnotic beat of her pendulum clock on the wall ticking the meaningless hours away.

I was enjoying the luxuries of a rustic nineteenth-century boyhood, but for the women Morrisonville life had few rewards. . . .

For baths, laundry, and dishwashing, they hauled buckets of water from a spring at the foot of a hill. To heat it, they chopped kindling to fire their wood stoves. They boiled laundry in tubs, scrubbed it on washboards until knuckles were raw, and wrung it out by hand. Ironing was a business of lifting heavy metal weights heated on the stove top. They scrubbed floors on hands and knees, thrashed rugs with carpet beaters, killed and plucked their own chickens, baked bread and pastries, grew and canned their own vegetables, patched the family's clothing on treadle-operated sewing machines, deloused the chicken coops, preserved fruits, picked potato bugs and tomato worms to protect their garden crop, darned stockings, made jelly and relishes, rose before the men to start the stove for breakfast and pack lunch pails, polished the chimneys of kerosene lamps, and even found time to tend the geraniums, hollyhocks, nasturtiums, dahlias, and peonies that grew around every house. By the end of a summer day a Morrisonville woman had toiled like a serf.

At sundown the men drifted back from the fields exhausted and steaming. They scrubbed themselves in enamel basins and, when supper was eaten, climbed up onto Ida Rebecca's porch to watch the night arrive. Presently the women joined them, and the twilight music of Morrisonville began:

The swing creaking, rocking chairs whispering on the porch planks, voices murmuring approval of the sagacity of Uncle Irvey as he quietly observed for probably the ten-thousandth time in his life, "A man works from sun to sun, but woman's work is never done."

Ida Rebecca, presiding over the nightfall

from the cane rocker, announcing, upon hearing of some woman "up there along the mountain" who had dropped dead hauling milk to the creamery, that "man is born to toil, and woman is born to suffer."

The timelessness of it: Nothing new had been said on that porch for a hundred years. If one of the children threw a rock close to someone's window, Uncle Harry removed his farmer's straw hat, swabbed the liner with his blue bandanna, and spoke the wisdom of the ages to everyone's complete satisfaction by declaring, "Satan finds work for idle hands to do."

If I interrupted the conversation with a question, four or five adults competed to be

Women wear bonnets to shield the bright sun as they hang their wash out to catch the summer breezes.

the first to say, "Children are meant to be seen and not heard."

If one of my aunts mentioned the gossip about some woman "over there around Bollington" or "out there towards Hillsboro," she was certain to be silenced by a scowl from Ida Rebecca or Uncle Irvey and a reminder that "little pitchers have big ears."

I was listening to a conversation that had been going on for generations.

Someone had a sick cow.

The corn was "burning up" for lack of rain.

If the sheriff had arrested a local boy for shooting somebody's bull: "That boy never brought a thing but trouble to his mother, poor old soul." . . .

Ancient Aunt Zell, who lived "down there around Lucketts," had to be buried on a day "so hot the flowers all wilted before they could get her in the ground, poor old soul."

When the lamps were lit inside, someone was certain to say to the children, "Early to bed and early to rise makes a man healthy, wealthy, and wise." . . .

For occasional treats I was taken on the

I was listening to a conversation that had been going on for generations.

three-mile trip to Lovettsville and there had my first glimpse of urban splendors. The commercial center was Bernard Spring's general store, a dark cavernous treasure house packed with the riches of the earth. . . .

Nearby stood the Spring family's mansion, the most astonishing architectural monument I had ever seen, a huge white wedding cake of a building filled with stained glass and crowned with turrets and lightning rods. The whole business had been ordered from the Sears, Roebuck catalog and erected according to mail-order instructions. Since Mr. Spring insisted on top-of-the-line in all his dealings, Lovettsville could boast that it contained the finest house in the Sears, Roebuck warehouse. . . .

Beyond Lovettsville, on the outer edge of my universe, lay Brunswick. I first walked in that vision of paradise hand-in-hand with my father, and those visits opened my eyes to the vastness and wonders of life's possibilities. . . .

On those magic occasions when my father took me to Brunswick, the supreme delight was to have Uncle Lewis seat me on a board placed across the arms of his barber chair, crank me into the sky, and subject me to the pampered luxury of being clippered, snipped, and doused with heavy applications of Lucky Tiger or Jeris hair tonic, which left my hair plastered gorgeously to the sides of my head and sent me into the street reeking of aromatic delight.

After one such clipping I climbed a hill in Brunswick with my father to call at Uncle Tom's house. Though Uncle Tom was fourteen years older, my father loved and respected him above all his brothers. Maybe it was because he saw in Tom the blacksmith some shadow of the blacksmith father who died when my father was only ten. Maybe it was because Tom, living in such splendor with his indoor bathroom and his Essex, had escaped Morrisonville and prospered. Maybe it was for Tom's sweetness of character, which was unusual among Ida Rebecca's boys.

Uncle Tom was at work that day, but Aunt Goldie gave us a warm welcome. She was a delicate woman, not much bigger than my mother, with hair of ginger red, blue eyes, and a way of looking at you and turning her head suddenly this way and that which reminded me of an alert bird. She was also a notoriously fussy housekeeper, constantly battling railroad grime to preserve her house's reputation for not containing "a speck of dust anywhere in it." Before admitting us to her spotless kitchen, she had my father and me wipe our shoes on the doormat, then made a fuss about how sweet I smelled and how handsome I looked, then cut me a huge slab of pie.

My great joy in calling on Aunt Goldie was the opportunity afforded to visit the indoor bathroom, so naturally after polishing off the pie I pretended an urgent need to use the toilet. This was on the second floor and required a journey through the famously dust-free dining room and parlor, but Aunt Goldie understood. "Take your shoes off first so you don't track up the floor," she said. Which I did. "And don't touch anything in the parlor."

With this caution she admitted me to the sanctum of spotlessness. I trod across immaculate rugs and past dining room furniture, armchairs, side tables, a settee, like a soldier walking in a mine field. There would be no dust left behind if I could help it.

A small boy runs toward his Natick, Massachusetts, home.

At the top of the stairs lay the miracle of plumbing. Shutting the door to be absolutely alone with it, I ran my fingers along the smooth enamel of the bathtub and glistening faucet handles of the sink. The white majesty of the toilet bowl, through which gallons of water could be sent rushing by the slightest touch of a silvery lever, filled me with envy. A roll of delicate paper was placed beside it. Here was luxury almost too rich to be borne by anyone whose idea of fancy toiletry was Uncle Irvey's two-hole privy and a Montgomery Ward catalog.

After gazing upon it as long as I dared without risking interruption by a search party, I pushed the lever and savored the supreme moment when thundering waters emptied into the bowl and vanished with a mighty gurgle. It was the perfect conclusion to a trip to Brunswick.

DELIGHTFUL DIVERSIONS AT HOME

With most of America living in rural areas at the turn of the century, life at home was cherished. Families not only worked and prayed together, but they played together too. Gathering around the radio to listen to humorist Will Rogers or hear how the Lone Ranger saved the day was a favorite pastime of both young and old. And Father was likely to get down on the living room rug with young Junior to help him set up a Lionel train while Mother stitched a new rag doll for Susie. Home was truly a haven for all.

Children in days gone by enjoyed playing marbles, reading about Dick Tracy or Little Orphan Annie in the comics, and going to bed with their Teddy bears, named after America's own President Theodore Roosevelt. Although all little girls had a rag doll or two that their mothers made for them, lucky girls also had a Kewpie doll. The Kewpie doll craze began when artist Rose O'Neill sketched the charming babydoll for *Ladies' Home Journal.*

Sunday play for children was restricted to more subdued diversions of a religious nature, the most popular of which was a Noah's ark set. These hand-carved toys featured Noah and his family along with two of every creature the carver could imagine, and some animals invented from pure whimsy!

In 1900 Joshua Lionel Cowen put his inventiveness and delight with miniaturization together with electricity and built a toy train for a store advertisement. To Cowen's surprise the train quickly sold and the store ordered six more. Cowen began producing catalogs to sell his tiny locomotives, depots, and tunnels, and his business boomed. Soon, Lionel trains were running around sofas and coffee tables in countless living rooms throughout America.

As the popularity of radio rose throughout the 1920s, Americans embraced the talking box as a new kind of family hearth. Neighborhood restaurants even began broadcasting favorite shows in order to keep their customers. Advertisements for everything from Ovaltine to Pepsodent toothpaste vied for airtime in between the programs. Radio made news available to a wider audience and brought Americans in rural areas in touch with the city dwellers. Even President Franklin Delano Roosevelt used radio to reach the masses in his "fireside chats."

As the familiar strains of the William Tell Overture filled the living room, families quickly gathered to hear the latest adventure of their favorite hero, the Lone Ranger, and his trusty companion, Tonto. Debuting in 1933, "The Lone Ranger" reigned as America's best-loved Western for twenty-two years. Other favorite radio shows included "The Shadow," "Amos 'n' Andy," and a game show called "Quiz Kids."

THE CALENDAR
OF CHILDHOOD

Carol Bessent Hayman

I remember the yearly calendar in the lovely season of childhood: the opening of the heart, the sweet unfolding of the tender flower, the slow passing of days, the changing scene, the coming of age. In my hometown, a small seacoast town in the nineteen thirties, in the big yellow house on the corner, this is how I remember it.

Ours was a quiet way of life, and the things I knew and loved were quiet things: the swing on the big shady porch, the easy chair in the living room with the book I was reading tucked under the cushion, the summer dusk that was soft as a fairy's wing with the sky all saffron and pink and rose, the hours on the breakwater looking out at the horizon with my heart full of dreams.

The summers stand out the brightest in my memory. The months were filled with long sunny days, the blue sound water beckoning me to come for a swim and a magic carpet of books available to while away the hours. My bedroom window overlooked the breakwater and sound, and I could lie on my bed and watch the slim white sailboats catching the breeze and see the wet, brown swimmers splashing about.

The autumns of my childhood never seemed to stay long. Indian summer lasted into October and even November with cool nights and warm days. The elm and oak trees shed their red and gold and brown, and the leaves made a whispering sound as they scuttled along the sidewalks that stretched along our street. Smoke rose from bonfires, and the air was heady with the pungent smell. Darkness began to fall earlier, and mothers hurried their children indoors and out of the chilly air. Suddenly one morning we awoke to frost and wintry

> *The leaves made a whispering sound as they scuttled along the sidewalks that stretched along our street.*

winds, and on my way out the door to school I noticed the Christmas catalogs lying in a convenient spot for Mama to start her Christmas shopping. Everything was always ordered, even the Christmas candies, and there was great delight in the weeks that lay ahead as I watched for the packages to arrive.

Winters were both the most difficult and the most exciting of seasons. Our house was large and the rooms (except for the kitchen and sitting room) unheated. All the hot water for baths, shampoos, and dishes had to be heated in a kettle on the kitchen stove. When Saturday bath time arrived, my sister and I took turns using a small wash tub in front of the wood burning stove with the doors closed and shades drawn. . . . On winter nights, the bed sheets were like layers of ice, and in the morning the tile floor was so cold that I feared my feet would stick to it. But the frigid days of December always brought Christmas—the bright spot in the winter calendar. How I loved the music, the fragrance, the lights, the excitement.

Soon spring would arrive, usually bright and blowy and filled with sunny skies and salty breezes. The daffodils were out in yellow dress, and I threw off coat and sweater with reckless abandon as I ran toward the summer days ahead.

Over and over the calendar repeated itself, taking me further and further away from the happy land of childhood. It changed me, molding me with the beautiful, never-to-be-forgotten days that now remain ever bright in my calendar of memories.

[My daughter] is going to Granny's for a week's visit. Home to the house I grew up in and love. Home to the big rooms, the shady

The sight and smell of burning leaves greet two neighborhood boys.

porch, the cool upstairs bedrooms, and the yard full of old-fashioned flowers. . . .

Home to the big rooms, the shady porch, the cool upstairs bedrooms, and the yard full of old-fashioned flowers.

I remember each tree that lined the three blocks I walked to downtown (two blocks to church). I remember the smell of supper cooking when I entered the front door, the welcome aroma of pork chops and grits and berry pie, or ham and scrambled eggs, and how it felt to snuggle deep in a chair with a good book while the quiet summer afternoon slipped into evening. I remember practicing the piano as dusk closed in and the notes went ringing across yards to neighbors watering plants or cutting grass or just standing talking about the weather.

A front porch beckons family members to its shade.

I remember being a little girl of three or four and sitting in a small oak rocking chair. Mama would put this little chair right in front of her own big rocking chair and sit with her foot on the round of my chair pushing it as she rocked back and forth. Over and over she would sing "The Old, Old Story,"

"The Ninety and Nine," and "Jesus Loves Me" and "Rock of Ages." I knew them long before I knew my ABC's. Along with the songs, and more than the music or motion as we rocked there together, was Mama's unwavering faith. Her calm, sweet voice singing the words of strength and courage was like a benediction; a blessed warmth covered us and hours passed. Neither Mama's foot on my chair nor her voice faltered. Unschooled, unlearned though she was, she offered me a real sense of music appreciation because of love's association. Always I will remember with a grateful heart the times when Mama pulled my little chair up to hers and began to rock and sing.

I remember the porch at night with its comfortable rockers and the street light aglow across the way for company. The warm, friendly voices passing and saying "Hello," "Hot today," or "Paper says rain tomorrow."

I remember climb-ing the stairs to my room and kneeling by my open window to say my prayers. The stars were very large and very clear, and the sea breeze touched my cheek.

If I had only known how good it all was. Oh, to go back again.

A cozy Victorian room offers an escape from the summer heat.

A Memory

When I am old, and dreaming by the fire,
One memory I'll keep until the close.
A little yard where honeysuckle grows,
A house whose walls surround my heart's desire.

A porch, well-guarded by twin maple trees,
A lighted window and an old arm chair,
A row of books, a gently sloping stair,
The scent of roses, on the summer breeze.

One memory I'll keep, and never tire,
A little house, a friendly maple tree,
And by the open fire, your smile for me —
When I am old, and dreaming by the fire!

Anne Campbell

Nostalgia

When we are straying dreamily
Along the paths of Memory —
It is the thoughts of home that start
The deepest yearnings of the heart.

For home is where our hearts belong.
A word, a picture or a song
Can strike a chord that brings to mind
The things that we have left behind.

A strange power binds us to our own.
And when we're exiled and alone
There comes this feeling, sharp as pain:
The longing to be home again.

Patience Strong

Now, Be a Little Lady

LaReine Warden Clayton

A bout once or twice a year Mother went down to St. Louis to shop. There was an early-morning excursion train that got into the city before the stores opened and then came back home before the family had gone to bed.

Often Mother would be asked to buy for many of the neighbors, for the big-city stores in conjunction with the railroads would offer bargain prices for the day, and neighbors bought for one another. . . .

Those were the days of homemade cotton underwear for little girls and ladies, of blouses and nightshirts for little boys, and long nightshirts and sometimes even dress shirts for men.

Every spring and fall the sewing woman came to our house for a week of sewing, or longer if Blossom and Sudie were at home. I think she charged fifty cents a day, and later five dollars a week. In making the underwear there were miles upon miles of tucks and ruffles. It would have been scandalous to make a plain petticoat or a pair of drawers, without the customary three or five tucks above a lace or embroidered ruffle, or to have a nightgown without a yoke of tucks between insets of embroidery or lace. All this, to say nothing of cotton dresses and woolen dresses and an occasional silk dress (only the very best of which were made for me by Mother alone, or for Mother by her dressmaker). Besides these spring and fall sewing orgies, Mother's sewing machine was never idle a week in the year, for there were ankle-length kitchen aprons to make and pillow slips and bolster cases and innumerable other household sewing. There was no money to spare for ready-made things, even if our stores had stocked them. Mother practiced every economy known to woman except doing without a cook. That she could never do.

There were materials of all kinds to be brought back from the city, and white long cloth—cambric, muslin, even sheeting—by the bolt, and an occasional bolt of good white cotton "Cloth of Gold" for Aunt

Every spring and fall the sewing woman came to our house for a week of sewing.

Dinah's or Aunt Frances's long white aprons. I was given the fancy seals from off these bolts of materials, and I still remember their trade names. Mother's

These entertainers are dressed in the latest styles of their era.

I secretly thought, verged on being tacky) were more becoming. . . . The rich brown taffeta bows that under Mother's deft tying looked like big pompons, and the starchy black bows that I wore in winter, seemed very dashing; but pale blue was nothing but pale blue no matter how big the bow. Otherwise, I was quite well pleased with my clothes.

These were the days of bows—of ruffles and ribbons and bows. It was the Gibson-girl era. The long years. The decade of 1900–1910. The pre-Ziegfeld days. The days of the small waist, the round hips and bust, double-ruffled flounces, feather boas, pompadours, and Merry Widow hats. Belts came around the back into a "dip," and were anchored low in a V in front by a firm pinning to a firmer corset, and hips rolled out roundly on three sides. . . .

big redheaded brother who lived in St. Louis footed the bill for this large-scale buying of white goods and would take her down into the wholesale district to stock up on the staples. Once or twice I went with her into that different world of wholesale houses, and I still remember the strange orderliness of the great supply houses and the odors of new goods.

For me the *pièce de résistance* of Mother's shopping would be the collection of hair-ribbon remnants that she would bring back to me, and an occasional blue satin sash. She never brought pink or red. I would have traded almost anything I owned for a pink hair bow and sash, or a brilliant red one for winter. But I had red hair, and Mother thought the greens, blues, browns, or even black, and "the beautiful plaids" (plaids,

Under the window in the upstairs hall, just over the front door, was an enormous coffin-like, long dress-box that we called the long box. In summer the winter clothing was packed away with mothballs and twist tobacco, and in winter the summer clothes were stored there. Finally it became a general storage box for dresses and coats and bonnets and furs that might some day be made over. Every so often Mother would draw up a low chair and seat herself before the long box and, in the manner of a lady who had business to attend, would proceed to unlock the old chest.

Then she would call to me, "I am going through the long box, and you may watch me if you care to."

Did I? I knew by heart every treasure in both the long box and Mother's trunk. There

I knew by heart every treasure in Mother's trunk.

were the three or four pairs of tiny baby bootees in the small front pigeonholes in the top tray of her trunk. "These were George's when he was a baby," she'd say. "Just look how beautifully they were made. That is clocking up the side. They were made with the very finest thread and the tiniest of little knitting needles. Your grandmother made them." I always begged for them. "No," said Mother, "you may not have them for your doll. I'm saving them to give to George some day."

And in the bottom of the chest there were two great, heavy knit bedspreads. "Your grandmother died before she finished these. I want to have old Miss What's-her-name finish them some day. She is probably the only one in town who could knit like this. I think she could follow the pattern. It is quite intricate, and I never saw anyone but Mother undertake it." I could see all of these things before we even opened a lid.

In the long box were the dresses and shawls and bonnets of my grandmother. They were of somber hue, mostly black and not at all interesting to me. There was one sparkling little jet-trimmed cape I liked to put on and wear a few minutes. There were black-lace fans and one large black-silk one heavy with feather tips—probably coq—that I liked to play with. But my

grandmother's few clothes seemed very dead indeed and even in life had had nothing more than an old-ladyish rustle to them.

The prize things in this box were three of Mother's best dresses. One was her going-away dress when she married Father. She always told me the story of it whenever she took it out.

"This was my going-away dress when I married your father! I went down to St. Louis and bought the material at Scruggs Vandevoort and Barney. They had imported it for Miss Madeleine Somebody and it was twelve dollars a yard. I took nine yards of it and paid Mrs. Brooks thirty-five dollars to make it up. It was a beautiful dress."

It was a beautiful dress. The material was moss-green silk, "heavy enough to stand alone." Woven into it were cut velvet leaves of a richer green. Pink-satin veins ran through each velvet leaf. The small buttons were of French enamel in the same shade of green, with little sprays of pink flowers on them to match the dress material. The sleeves were slashed, and exposed the under puffing of delicate pink silk. This and the pink-silk guimpe were accordion-pleated. There was a small collar of real lace at the neck. The whole dress, skirt and all, was lined and boned. Years later Mother decided to have it ripped up and made over, but for some reason she never did. She took scraps of the material, however, and made each of her three children needle books with covers of this material. She gave one to Hu and one to George, but I do not think she ever gave me mine.

My favorite was a black satin trimmed

with jet. Unlike the dead-black clothes of my grandmother, this dress had life and sparkle and an authentic air of style that never left it even in its tomblike chest. Mother loved it—so did I—and she lifted it proudly.

"I had this when I was a widow!" she said.

"A widow" sounded very stylish, I thought.

"I saw the picture in Harper's Bazaar. It was a picture of the Duchess of Marlborough in the dress she wore to something, and I decided right then and there that I wanted it copied. I cut the picture out and drew the rest of it in detail and sent it down to Minnie Baker in Louisville, Kentucky—your brother George's Aunt Minnie—and told her exactly what I wanted, and she got it! Then I took the picture and the materials out to Mrs. Brooks, and she made it up for me. I had plenty of money in those days! And I was quite extravagant." That was one of the few times I ever heard Mother mention money.

"I never had as many compliments on a dress in my life! I wore it in Washington City and had my picture taken in it. It's a very handsome dress! I drew a pattern for that jet yoke in detail myself, and bit by bit the jet was worked up into it over a foundation. It's the set of the yoke down over the shoulders that made the dress. I stayed at the old National Hotel in Washington City where

In 1925, advertisements popularized the flapper style.

your grandparents spent their honeymoon. Your grandmother's cousins owned that hotel even then, and I visited them there and wore this dress. Your father has the picture of me in it." I knew the picture, too. Mother held her head like a queen and looked every inch the patrician that, indeed, she was. I wonder what ever became of that dress!

Then there was the blue-wool crepe-barege; a material veil-thin, like a crepy wool chiffon. This, too, was made by Mrs. Brooks, the dressmaker par excellence. It was of royal blue made over very rustly silk taffeta, with just a touch of a train. It was trimmed with open-work "wheels" of green-silk banding and piped in green satin. With this she wore little green kid gloves—size 5½—and a tiny hat of blue panne velvet trimmed with curly ostrich tips. Mother spoke of that hat lovingly as "my little toque." I think Mother wore that dress for ten years, and it always had an air and a dash of style. I still have the little green kid gloves. They are old and stiff now, and I found them packed away with Father's white-kid wedding gloves in Mother's trunk.

There were other dresses that I remember, for even as a child I loved clothes and noticed them in detail. Even the materials now long since dropped from fashion, I remember.

Home Sweet Home

JOHN HOWARD PAYNE

HENRY ROWLEY BISHOP

1. 'Mid plea - sures and pal - a - ces though I may roam,
2. An ex - ile from home, splen - dor daz - zles in vain,
3. To thee, I'll re - turn, o - ver bur - dened with care,

Be it ev - er so hum - ble, there's no place like home;
Oh, give me my low - ly thatched cot - tage a - gain;
The heart's dear - est sol - ace will smile on me there.

A charm from the sky seems to hal - low us
The birds sing - ing gai - ly, that come at my
No more from that cot - tage a - gain will I

"Be it ever so humble, there's no place like home."

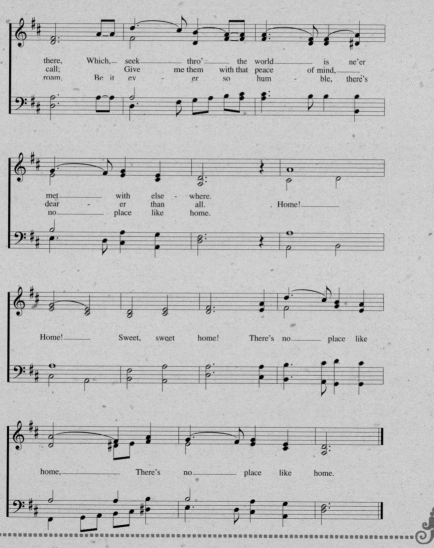

there,   Which,   seek   thro'   the   world   is   ne'er
call;   Give   me   them   with that   peace   of   mind,
roam,   Be   it   ev   -   er   so   hum   -   ble,   there's

met   with   else -   where.   Home!
dear   -   er   than   all.
no   place   like   home.

Home!   Sweet,   sweet   home!   There's   no   place   like

home,   There's   no   place   like   home.

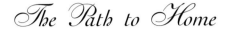

The Path to Home

There's the mother at the doorway, and the children at the gate,
And the little parlor windows with the curtains white and straight.
There are shaggy asters blooming in the bed that lines the fence,
And the simplest of the blossoms seems of mighty consequence.
Oh, there isn't any mansion underneath God's starry dome
That can rest a weary pilgrim like the little place called home.

Men have sought for gold and silver; men have dreamed at night of fame;
In the heat of youth they've struggled for achievement's honored name;
But the selfish crowns are tinsel, and their shining jewels paste,
And the wine of pomp and glory soon grows bitter to the taste.
For there's never any laughter, howsoever far you roam,
Like the laughter of the loved ones in the happiness of home.

There is nothing so important as the mother's lullabies,
Filled with peace and sweet contentment, when the moon begins to rise—
Nothing real except the beauty and the calm upon her face
And the shouting of the children as they scamper round the place.
For the greatest of man's duties is to keep his loved ones glad
And to have his children glory in the father they have had.

So where'er a man may wander, and whatever be his care,
You'll find his soul still stretching to the home he left somewhere.
You'll find his dreams all tangled up with hollyhocks in bloom,
And the feet of little children that go racing through a room,
With the happy mother smiling as she watches them at play—
These are all in life that matter, when you've stripped the rest away.

Edgar A. Guest

An antique chair and heirloom lace linens recall a past day.

GIVE ME AN
OLD-FASHIONED PEDDLER

Marjorie Holmes

*S*ign of age though it may be, it seems to me that solicitors and salesmen somehow lack the appeal and flavor they had when I was a smalltown child. Today when my door chimes echo their insistent summons above the drumming of the shower, what do I find when I grab a robe and dash dripping to the door? A lace lady? A scissors grinder? A chimney sweep? Maybe a gypsy, even?

No, indeed.

I'm rewarded by a neighbor collecting for another fund. Or a feverish if beaming phony, claiming he must have my magazine subscriptions within the hour or he'll lose a scholarship to college. A nicely scrubbed little boy clutching tickets to the Cub Scout circus. The Fuller Brush man maybe. The Avon lady or a soulful pitchman for cemetery lots.

The fact that I don't relish these interruptions puzzles my children. With the eternal kindness and curiosity of the young, they'd have me invite the stranger in and send no one away without having first lightened my purse.

They don't realize that, despite all our "time-saving" gadgets and contrivances, today's mothers are actually busier in many ways than were their grandmothers. Also, though most communities have laws that attempt to license and thus eliminate many canvassers, we are still besieged by more people in a week's span than our mothers might have seen in a summer.

In my hometown each day stretched out before the housewife pretty much like the day before. She was glad to pause in her often horrendous labors (scrubbing on a washboard, say, or whaling the daylights out of a rug) and pass the time of day with a peddler while examining his wares. Those who came calling door-to-door—whether regulars like the Jewel Tea man and old blind Mr. Clarke, who sold soap, or the occasional stranger with brooms over his shoulder—were treated like welcome guests.

"Oh, my goodness, here comes the Jewel Tea wagon," my mother would exclaim. "Pick up those papers quick, and just look at this floor!"

Mr. Hix, the Jewel Tea man, didn't seem to notice, sitting at the oilcloth-covered kitchen table, drinking coffee, and passing along gossipy items picked up on his peregrinations, while Mother scribbled additional items on her list. We usu-

Those who came calling door-to-door were treated like welcome guests.

ally trailed him out to his "wagon," which was actually a skinny-wheeled, top-heavy truck. But, to our dazzled eyes and nostrils, its dusky interior, fragrant with spices, cocoa, tea, its air of plenitude and mobility, made it as enchanting as a desert caravan.

Mother, like many women, always had to rationalize what she bought. "Well, now yes, they are a little higher than the stores downtown, but it's so convenient. And they give such nice premiums."

The premiums were the pay-off—the real forerunner of today's trading stamps. She was saving her coupons for a fringed floor lamp.

Another regular was Mrs. Cannon, a large bosomy, rich-smelling woman who took orders for yard goods, ribbons, and lace. We called her the Lace Lady; she always wore fountains of it at her wrists and throat, or a lacy shirtwaist tucked into a crackling taffeta skirt. The bolts of lace she brought forth from her big black leather satchel and unwound before your eyes— thick creamy ecru stuff for the yokes of nightgowns or the bordering of curtains

and tablecloths; exquisite hand embroidery from the Philippines, or a delicate white froth, like snowflakes or spiderwebs.

Mrs. Cannon had jet-black hair— she went to Omaha to have it dyed, people said—a little moustache, furry eyebrows, and bright black friendly eyes. She was a little bit like a plump jolly spider herself, sitting there in her lovely webbed entanglements of lace. From her, Mother bought most of our broad, watered silk hair ribbons. Mrs. Cannon measured them thumb to nose, and slashed them off smartly with a pair of bright blunt scissors that danced at her waist. She then wound them about the sparkling spindles of her jeweled fingers. . . .

Every Saturday, regular as the clock on the Presbyterian church tower, a small boy would come leading Mr. Clarke and his tapping cane to

Neighbors are happy to pause from their workday and share the latest gossip.

the steps. One week to take your order, the next to deliver it. Nobody really cared much for his tarry-smelling brown shampoo or his white, faintly stinging hand soap. But "you just can't turn him away."

He was so sweet and kind and feeble and vaguely Biblical, a little child leading him like that. "Imagine going through life in the dark." We couldn't, even when we shut our eyes and groped about. . . .

It was the advent of a stranger, however, that really perked things up. A tramp at the back door was a matter of tender excitement and subtly delicious alarm. Little bells of adventure rang in our blood as Mother bade him join the family for a square meal, or if he were unduly dirty and suspicious, fed him feeling guilty and unchristian, on the back steps.

Front porches were perfect spots to hear a peddler's pitch.

We could feel (often smell!) the open roads, the campfires, the boxcars rumbling through the night while a train whistle hooted its wild mysterious call. Moved, we would watch him trudge humbly off, sometimes in an old coat Mother had dug from the closet, clutching a dollar bill Dad had forked over.

"We can't spare it, but doggone it, I just couldn't bear not to," Dad would say, looking sheepish but glowing. And we'd glow too, sharing the exaltation.

On a rare and memorable occasion we'd have a chimney sweep. . . . Elfish-looking little men in tall, pointed hats, their white smiles slashing their sooty faces, gay and a bit terrifying.

They would go squirreling onto a roof and disappear into the chimney, probing and prodding with their devilish-looking instruments. The chimneys, clotted from years of wood and coal smoke, would rain down their velvety black accumulation.

You couldn't invite them in, they were too grimy. But you carried a pitcher of ice water or lemonade to cool them after their labors, and they quaffed it with mighty workings of their Adam's apples. Then off they'd go, dark imps that had added a dash to the day. . . .

Less spectacular but always diverting were the men who sharpened knives and scissors on their portable grinding wheels. And the genteel young ladies who took orders for the *Book of Knowledge*. Commonplace but perhaps jolliest of all were the broom peddlers.

"Brooms for sale . . . nice, new brooms!" the broom peddler would call, humping along under the burden of his heavy, bright bouquet. He carried them over his shoulder, those homely wheat-colored whiskery flowers. And what a fine business he did.

The money was counted out and the man trudged on. There you were with the new broom smelling dry and oaty, to be straddled and ridden, making a fine swish, and leaking a few loose golden strands across the floor.

Your mother would dubiously try it out, struggling with its frisky newness like a horse to be trained. Her eyes would have a kind of wistful twinkling as she said, "It's funny, but I sort of hate to break in a new broom—you get so used to the old one."

You knew what she meant. There was something almost human about a broom. The new one occupied the position of prestige on the hook behind the kitchen door; the old one—lopsided, worn down but dependable—was demoted now to porch or sidewalk sweeping, or the brushing off of snowy boots come wintertime. You hoped the old one didn't mind . . .

Some things never change. We had then, as now, the perennial parade of small boys and girls selling seeds and postcards and subscriptions (and took our own exciting turns at the ringing of doorbells). Before long we began to have our Fuller Brush men, our Avon ladies, our assaults of young people "working their way" through colleges that have never

heard of them. Gradually, something began to be missing, there I'm sure as well as here in suburbia today; the flavor and juice of the old-time interruptions. The sense of expectation, welcome, and surprise. But most of all, a sense of personal involvement with these briefly passing lives.

My children, however eager, can't really enjoy seeing me cope with all these people, as I proclaim in some desperation: "No, no, I cannot use any more brushes, beauty products, magazines, or cemetery lots."

I'd like to fling open the door some day and find a genuine blind man tapping up the steps. Or an old-fashioned smelly hobo to be fed and warmed and sent on his way . . . Or a lady with ribbons and laces . . . A peddler of brooms—a chimney sweep!

Though his vehicle has changed, the ice-cream truck has always been a welcome sight.

FEEDING THE FAMILY

Before the days of fast-food restaurants and take-out pizza, feeding the family was a time-consuming task. At the end of the nineteenth century, Americans had yet to learn the pleasures of such modern-day staples as canned baby food, frozen foods, and, yes, the candy bar. But wise inventors and America's sweet tooth were soon to produce a tastier diet that reflected the country's tradition of eating well.

The company synonymous with baby food all started when Daniel F. Gerber became impatient waiting for his wife to prepare dinner for the couple's young daughter. The year was 1927, and a mother's only choices for feeding her infant were expensive prescription-only baby food or the tedious task of mashing food herself, thrice daily. Gerber teamed with his family's canning company to produce and market a new line of baby food that was tasty, nutritious, and economical. The Gerber Products Company was born, and within one year, babies had consumed tens of thousands of jars of strained vegetables and fruits.

Already a success in the candy business, Milton Hershey's place in chocolate history was secured after he was introduced to chocolate-making machinery at the 1893 World's Columbian Exposition. By the next year, Hershey had created and was producing the first candy bars.

After Hershey's success, competitors were soon following suit: the Tootsie Roll was first introduced in 1896, the Baby Ruth (named not for the baseball player, but for Grover Cleveland's daughter) in 1920, and Oh Henry! bars in 1921.

Before the days of electric refrigeration began in the 1930s, keeping food fresh and crisp was a daily challenge, and the kitchen icebox was the answer. Ice harvesting (pictured below) was a difficult, yet profitable business, involving hacking and sawing ice from frozen lakes, then storing and shipping it. The iceman, delivering from door to door, made his rounds several days a week, using iron tongs to hoist sixty-pound blocks of ice from his brightly painted horse-drawn wagon to his customers' kitchens.

"ITS SO SIMPLE"

JELL-O
America's most famous dessert

THE great merit of Jell-O is that it is always ready. It is made as easily as a cup of tea is brewed. Write for a free booklet describing a wide variety of uses.

The GENESEE PURE FOOD COMPANY, Le Roy, New York
Canadian Factory, at Bridgeburg, Ontario

In 1892, lawyer Henry Perky was impressed by a fellow hotel patron's breakfast: a bowlful of boiled wheat and milk. Told it aided the stranger's digestion, Perky tried some himself and returned home to Denver with thoughts of shredded wheat in his head. He began peddling pillow-shaped biscuits of wheat from door to door. In 1901, Perky built a bakery near Niagara Falls and offered tourists free samples of his new breakfast food. Shredded wheat was soon on tables across the country.

Even MARK TWAIN *would have been stumped!*

THE great humorist said that cauliflower is cabbage with a college education. What would he, what could he, have said about the yummies which Campbell's develop to such glorious perfection for the making of tomato soup?

And if the tomatoes would have taxed his powers of adequate description, what of the soup itself? For Campbell's Tomato Soup, with all its individual tang and flavor, is hard indeed to put into words.

Just let it speak for itself—to your appetite and your delight in exhilarating goodness. If ever a soup appealed to your taste as being in a class by itself, this is it. "I don't know why—it is so delicious or how to describe it," you will say, "but I do know that it is the soup for me!"

Tomato Soup when you add water. Cream of Tomato when you add milk. An irresistible delight either way!

Double rich! Double strength!
Campbell's Soups being concentrated require the addition of an equal quantity of water to your kitchen, you obtain twice the quantity of soup at the same cost.

21 kinds to choose from:

CAMPBELL'S TOMATO SOUP

BREAD AND BUTTONHOLES

Louisa May Alcott

*W*hat in the world is my girl thinking about all alone here, with such a solemn face?" asked Dr. Alec, coming into the study, one November day, to find Rose sitting there with folded hands and a very thoughtful aspect.

"Uncle, I want to have some serious conversation with you, if you have time," she said, coming out of a brown study, as if she had not heard his question.

"I'm entirely at your service, and most happy to listen," he answered, in his politest manner, for when Rose put on her womanly little airs he always treated her with a playful sort of respect that pleased her very much.

Now, as he sat down beside her, she said, very soberly, "I've been trying to decide what trade I would learn, and I want you to advise me."

"Trade, my dear?" and Dr. Alec looked so astonished that she hastened to explain.

"I forgot that you didn't hear the talk about it up at Cosey Corner. You see we used to sit under the pines and sew, and talk a great deal—all the ladies, I mean—and I liked it very much. Mother Atkinson thought that everyone should have a trade, or something to make a living out of, for rich people may grow poor, you know, and poor people have to work. Her girls were very clever, and could do ever so many things, and Aunt Jessie thought the old lady was right; so when I saw how happy and independent those young ladies were, I wanted to have a trade, and then it wouldn't matter about money, though I like to have it well enough."

In the good old-fashioned way she is very accomplished, and has made this house a happy home.

Dr. Alec listened to this explanation with a curious mixture of surprise, pleasure, and amusement in his face, and looked at his little niece as if she had suddenly changed into a young woman. . . .

"I quite agree with the ladies, and shall be glad to help you decide on something if I can," said the Doctor seriously. "What do you incline to? A natural taste or talent is a great help in choosing, you know."

"I haven't any talent, or any especial taste that I can see, and that is why I can't decide, Uncle. So, I think it would be a good plan to pick out some very useful business and learn it, because I don't do it for pleasure, you see, but as a part of my education, and to be ready in case I'm ever poor," answered Rose, looking as if she rather longed for a little poverty so that her useful gift might be exercised.

"Well, now, there is one very excellent, necessary, and womanly accomplishment that no girl should be without, for it is a help to rich and poor, and the comfort of families depends upon it. This fine talent is neglected nowadays, and considered old-fashioned, which is a sad mistake, and one that I don't mean to make in bringing up my girl. It should be a part of every girl's education, and I know of a most accomplished lady who will teach you in the best and pleasantest manner."

"Oh, what is it?" cried Rose eagerly, charmed to be met in this helpful and cordial way.

"Housekeeping!" answered Dr. Alec.

"Is that an accomplishment?" asked Rose, while her face fell, for she had indulged in all sorts of vague, delightful dreams.

"Yes; it is one of the most beautiful as well as useful of all the arts a woman can learn. Not so romantic, perhaps, as singing, painting, writing, or teaching, even; but one that makes many

Helping in the kitchen was a familiar rite of passage for young girls.

happy and comfortable, and home the sweetest place in the world. Yes, you may open your big eyes; but it is a fact that I had rather see you a good housekeeper than the greatest belle in the city. It need not interfere with any talent you may possess, but it is a necessary part of your training, and I hope that you will set about it at once, now that you are well and strong."

"Who is the lady?" asked Rose, rather impressed by her uncle's earnest speech.

"Aunt Plenty."

"Is she accomplished?" began Rose in a

wondering tone, for this great-aunt of hers had seemed the least cultivated of them all.

"In the good old-fashioned way she is very accomplished, and has made this house a happy home to us all, ever since we can remember. She is not elegant, but genuinely good, and so beloved and respected that there will be universal mourning for her when her place is empty. . . . "

"I should like to have people feel so about me. Can she teach me to do what she does, and to grow as good?" asked Rose, with a little prick of remorse for even thinking that Aunt Plenty was a commonplace old lady.

"Yes, if you don't despise such simple lessons as she can give. I know it would fill her dear old heart with pride and pleasure to feel that anyone cared to learn of her, for she fancies her day gone by. Let her teach you how to be what she has been—a skillful, frugal, cheerful housewife; the maker and the keeper of a happy home, and by and by you will see what a valuable lesson it is."

"I will, Uncle. But how shall I begin?"

"I'll speak to her about it, and she will make it all right with Dolly, for cooking is one of the main things, you know."

"So it is! I don't mind that a bit, for I like to mess, and used to try at home; but I had no one to tell me, so I never did much but spoil my aprons. Pies are great fun, only Dolly is so

cross, I don't believe she will ever let me do a thing in the kitchen."

"Then we'll cook in the parlor. I fancy Aunt Plenty will manage her, so don't be troubled. Only mind this, I'd rather you learned how to make good bread than the best pies ever baked. When you bring me a handsome, wholesome loaf, entirely made by yourself, I shall be more pleased than if you offered me a pair of slippers embroidered in the very latest style. I don't wish to bribe you, but I'll give you my heartiest kiss, and promise to eat every crumb of the loaf myself."

"It's a bargain! It's a bargain! Come and tell Auntie all about it, for I'm in a hurry to begin," cried Rose, dancing before him toward the parlor, where Miss Plenty sat alone knitting contentedly, yet ready to run at the first call for help of any sort, from any quarter.

No need to tell how surprised and gratified she was at the invitation she received to teach the child the domestic arts which were her only accomplishments, nor to relate how energetically she set about her pleasant task. . . .

To tell the truth, the elder aunts had sometimes felt that they did not have quite their share of the little niece who had won their hearts long ago, and was the sunshine of the house. They talked it over together sometimes, but always ended by saying that as Alec had all the responsibility, he should have the larger share of the dear girl's love and time, and they would be contented with such crumbs of comfort as they could get.

Dr. Alec had found out this little secret, and, after reproaching himself for being blind and selfish, was trying to devise some way of mending matters without troubling anyone, when Rose's new whim suggested an excellent method of weaning her a little from himself. He did not know how fond he was of her till he gave her up to the new teacher, and often could not resist peeping in at the door, to see how she got on, or stealing sly looks through the slide when she was deep in dough, or listening intently to some impressive lecture from Aunt Plenty. They caught him at it now and then, and ordered him off the premises at the point of the rolling-pin; or, if unusually successful, and, therefore, in a milder mood, they lured him away with bribes of gingerbread, a stray pickle, or a tart that was not quite symmetrical enough to suit their critical eyes.

Of course he made a point of partaking copiously of all the delectable messes that now appeared at table, for both the cooks were on their mettle, and he fared sumptuously every day. But an especial relish was given to any dish when, in reply to his honest praise of it, Rose colored up with innocent pride, and said modestly,

"I made that, Uncle, and I'm glad you like it."

It was some time before the perfect loaf appeared, for bread-making is an art not easily learned. . . . It appeared at tea-time, on a silver salver, proudly borne in by Phoebe, who could not refrain from whispering, with a beaming face, as she set it down before Dr. Alec,

"Ain't it just lovely, sir?"

"It is a regularly splendid loaf! Did my girl make it all herself?" he asked, surveying the shapely, sweet-smelling object, with real interest and pleasure.

"Every particle herself, and never asked a bit of help or advice from anyone," answered Aunt Plenty, folding her hands with an air of unmitigated satisfaction, for her pupil certainly did her great credit.

"I've had so many failures and troubles that I really thought I never should be able to do it alone. Dolly let one splendid batch burn up because I forgot it. She was there and smelt it, but never did a thing, for she said, when I undertook to bake bread I must give my whole mind to it. Wasn't it hard? She might have called me at least," said Rose, recollecting, with a sigh, the anguish of that moment. . . .

"Never mind her now, but tell me all about

He made a point of partaking copiously of all the delectable messes that now appeared at table.

my loaf," said Dr. Alec. . . .

"There's nothing to tell, Uncle, except that I did my best, gave my mind to it, and sat watching over it all the while it was in the oven till I was quite baked myself. Everything went right this time, and it came out a nice, round, crusty loaf, as you see. Now taste it, and tell me if it is good as well as handsome."

"Must I cut it? Can't I put it under a glass cover and keep it in the parlor as they do wax flowers and fine works of that sort?"

"What an idea, Uncle! It would mould and be spoilt. Besides, people would laugh at us, and make fun of my old-fashioned accomplishment. You promised to eat it, and you must; not all at once, but as soon as you can, so I can make you some more."

Dr. Alec solemnly cut off his favorite crusty slice, and solemnly ate it; then wiped his lips, and brushing back Rose's hair, solemnly kissed her on the forehead, saying heartily,

The busy needles were embroidering all sorts of bright patterns on the lives of the workers.

"My dear, it is perfect bread, and you are an honor to your teacher. When we have our model school I shall offer a prize for the best bread, and you will get it."

"I've got it already, and I'm quite satisfied," said Rose, slipping into her seat, and trying to hide her right hand which had a burn on it.

But Dr. Alec saw it, guessed how it came there, and after tea insisted on easing the pain which she would hardly confess.

"Aunt Clara says I am spoiling my hands, but I don't care, for I've had such good times with Aunt Plenty, and I think she has enjoyed it as much as I have. Only one thing troubles me, Uncle, and I want to ask you about it," said Rose, as they paced up and down the hall in the twilight, the bandaged hand very carefully laid on Dr. Alec's arm.

"More little confidences? I like them immensely, so tell away, my dear."

"Well, you see I feel as if Aunt Peace would like to do something for me, and I've found out what it can be. You know she can't go about like Auntie Plen, and we are so busy nowadays that she is rather lonely, I'm afraid. So I want to take lessons in sewing of her. She works so beautifully, and it is a useful thing, you know, and I ought to be a good needlewoman as well as housekeeper, oughtn't I?"

"Bless your kind little heart, that is what I was thinking of the other day when Aunt Peace said she saw you very seldom now, you were so busy. I wanted to speak of it, but fancied you had as much on your hands as you could manage. It would delight the dear woman to teach you all her delicate handicraft, especially buttonholes, for I believe that is where young ladies fail; at least I've heard them say so. So, do you devote your mind to buttonholes; make 'em all over my clothes if you want something to practice on. I'll wear any quantity."

Rose laughed at this reckless offer, but promised to attend to that important branch, though she confessed that darning was her weak point. Whereupon Uncle Alec engaged to supply her with socks in all stages of dilapidation, and to have a new set at once, so that she could run the heel for him as a pleasant beginning.

Then they went up to make their request in due form, to the great delight of gentle Aunt Peace, who got quite excited with the fun that went on while they wound yarn, looked up darning-needles, and fitted out a nice little mending basket for her pupil.

Very busy and very happy were Rose's days now, for in the morning she went about the house with Aunt Plenty attending to linen closets and storerooms, pickling and preserving, exploring garret and cellar to see that all was right, and learning, in the good old-fashioned manner, to look well after the ways of the household.

In the afternoon, after her walk or drive, she sat with Aunt Peace plying her needle, while Aunt Plenty, whose eyes were failing, knit and chatted briskly, telling many a pleasant story of old times, till the three were moved to laugh and cry together, for the busy needles were embroidering all sorts of bright patterns on the lives of the workers, though they seemed to be only stitching cotton and darning hose.

It was a pretty sight to see the rosy-faced little maid sitting between the two old ladies, listening dutifully to their instructions, and cheering the lessons with her lively chatter and blithe laugh. If the kitchen had proved attractive to Dr. Alec when Rose was there at work, the sewing-room was quite irresistible, and he made himself so agreeable that no one had the heart to drive him away, especially when he read aloud or spun yarns.

"There! I've made you a new set of warm nightgowns with four buttonholes in each. See if they are not neatly done," said Rose, one day, some weeks after the new lessons began.

"Even to a thread, and nice little bars across the end so I can't tear them when I twitch the buttons out. Most superior work, ma'am, and I'm deeply grateful; so much so, that I'll sew on these buttons myself, and save those tired fingers from another prick."

"You sew them on?" cried Rose, with her eyes wide open in amazement.

"Wait a bit till I get my sewing tackle, and then you shall see what I can do."

"Can he, really?" asked Rose of Aunt Peace, as Uncle Alec marched off with a comical air of importance.

"Oh, yes, I taught him years ago, before he went to sea; and I suppose he has had to do things for himself, more or less, ever since, so he has kept his hand in."

He evidently had, for he was soon back with a funny little work-bag, out of which he produced a thimble without a top; and, having threaded his needle, he proceeded to sew on the buttons so handily that Rose was much impressed and amused.

"I wonder if there is anything in the world that you cannot do," she said, in a tone of respectful admiration.

"There are one or two things that I am not up to yet," he answered, with a laugh in the corner of his eye, as he waxed his thread with a flourish.

"I should like to know what?"

"Bread and buttonholes, ma'am."

Young Alice Dorn enjoys her new electric sewing machine in this 1950 photograph.

HOME FOR THE HOLIDAYS

Oh, the excitement of the old-fashioned holidays, filled with handmade ornaments, wind-up toys, and puddings, pies, and sugarplums. Long ago, the family had to wait all year to enjoy such treats as turkey and dressing, and the approach of Christmas dinner was met with much anticipation.

❖ COUNTRY SWEET POTATO PIE (Makes one 9-inch pie)

 1 9-inch unbaked pastry crust (recipe follows)
1¼ cups cooked, mashed sweet potatoes
 ½ cup packed light-brown sugar
 ½ teaspoon salt
 ¼ teaspoon ground cinnamon
 ⅛ teaspoon ground nutmeg

 2 large eggs, lightly beaten
 ½ cup plain nonfat yogurt
 ¼ cup milk
 1 tablespoon butter, melted
12 pecan halves, for garnish
   Sweetened whipped cream

Preheat oven to 400° F. In a large bowl, combine mashed sweet potatoes, brown sugar, salt, cinnamon, and nutmeg; mix well. Stir in eggs, yogurt, milk, and melted butter. Pour potato mixture into the pastry crust. Arrange pecan halves on top of pie. Bake about 45 minutes or until a knife inserted in the center comes out clean and crust is golden. Remove to a wire rack to cool. Serve warm with a dollop of whipped cream on each serving.

❖ SUGAR COOKIES (Makes about 4 dozen 2-inch cookies)

 ⅓ cup butter
 ⅓ cup shortening
 2 cups all-purpose flour
 ¾ cup granulated sugar
 1 egg
 1 tablespoon milk
 1 teaspoon baking powder

 1 teaspoon vanilla
 ⅛ teaspoon salt
 1 cup sifted confectioners' sugar
 ¼ teaspoon vanilla
   Milk
   Food coloring if desired

In a large bowl, cream butter with shortening until fluffy. Gradually add half the flour. Stir in sugar, egg, milk, baking powder, vanilla, and salt. Stir to mix well. Stir in remaining flour. Divide dough in half; cover and chill a couple of hours or until easy to handle. Preheat oven to

275° F. On a lightly floured surface, roll out each half until approximately ⅛-inch thick. Cut into shapes with 2-inch cookie cutters. Place on an ungreased cookie sheet, about one inch apart. Bake 7 minutes or until cookie looks dry but edges are not brown. Remove to a wire rack to cool. In a small mixing bowl, combine sugar and vanilla. Stir in a tablespoon of milk. If necessary, stir in additional milk, a teaspoon at a time, until frosting is smooth and of desired consistency. If desired, divide frosting into small containers and tint with food coloring. Makes about ½ cup frosting.

EARLY AMERICAN GINGERBREAD (Makes 1 loaf)

- 2 cups all-purpose flour
- 1 teaspoon baking powder
- ½ teaspoon salt
- 1½ teaspoons ground ginger
- 1 teaspoon ground cinnamon
- ½ teaspoon ground allspice
- ¼ teaspoon ground cloves
- ¼ teaspoon ground nutmeg
- ½ cup butter, at room temperature
- ½ cup packed dark-brown sugar
- ½ cup unsulfured molasses
- ¼ cup honey
- 2 large eggs
- ½ cup sour cream
- 1 cup mashed ripe banana

Preheat oven to 350° F. Grease and lightly flour a 9-by-5-by-2¾-inch loaf pan. In a large bowl, sift together flour, baking powder, salt, ginger, cinnamon, allspice, cloves, and nutmeg. Set aside. In a large bowl, cream butter with brown sugar until fluffy. Add molasses and honey; mix until smooth. Add eggs, one at a time, mixing well after each. Stir in the sour cream and banana and mix until smooth. Gradually add dry ingredients, mix until just combined. Mound batter into pan and bake 55 to 60 minutes or until a toothpick inserted into the center comes out clean. Cool in pan on a wire rack 10 minutes. Run a knife around edges of the pan to loosen and turn bread out onto the rack. Serve warm.

PASTRY CRUST (Makes 1 pie crust)

- 1¼ cups all-purpose flour
- ½ teaspoon salt
- ⅓ cup shortening
- 3 to 4 tablespoons cold water

In a medium bowl, stir together flour and salt. Cut in shortening until pieces are the size of small peas. Sprinkle 1 tablespoon of the water over part of the mixture; gently toss with a fork. Push to side of bowl. Repeat until all is moistened. Form dough into a ball. On a lightly floured surface, flatten dough with hands. Roll from center to edge, forming a circle about 12 inches in diameter. Wrap pastry around rolling pin. Unroll into pie plate; trim edges. Bake as directed in individual recipe.

HOME FOR CHRISTMAS

Carson McCullers

*S*ometimes in August, weary of the vacant, boiling afternoon, my younger brother and sister and I would gather in the dense shade under the oak tree in the back yard and talk of Christmas and sing carols. Once after such a conclave, when the tunes of the carols still lingered in the heat-shimmered air, I remember climbing up into the tree-house and sitting there alone for a long time.

Brother called up: "What are you doing?"

"Thinking," I answered.

"What are you thinking about?"

"I don't know."

"Well, how can you be thinking when you don't know what you are thinking about?"

I did not want to talk with my brother. I was experiencing the first wonder about the mystery of Time. Here I was, on this August afternoon, in the tree-house, in the burnt, jaded yard, sick and tired of all our summer ways. . . . How could it be that I was I and now was now when in four months it would be Christmas, wintertime, cold weather, twilight and the glory of the Christmas tree? I puzzled about the *now* and *later* and rubbed the inside of my elbow until there was a little roll of dirt between my forefinger and thumb. Would the *now I* of the tree-house and the August afternoon be the same *I* of winter, firelight and the Christmas tree? I wondered.

My brother repeated: "You say you are thinking but you don't know what you are thinking about. What are you really doing up there? Have you got some secret candy?" . . .

Christmas was nearer on the September Sunday that Daddy rounded us up in the car and drove us out on dusty country roads to pick elderberry blooms. . . . On November Sundays we went to the woods with a big basket of fried chicken dinner, thermos jug and coffee-pot. We hunted partridge berries in the pine woods near our town. These scarlet berries grew hidden underneath the glossy brown pine needles that lay in a slick carpet beneath the tall wind-singing trees. The bright berries were a Christmas decoration, lasting in water through the whole season.

In December the windows downtown were filled with toys, and my

A couple returns from the woods with their hand-cut Christmas tree.

brother and sister and I were given two dollars apiece to buy our Christmas presents. We patronized the ten-cent stores, choosing between jackstones, pencil boxes, water colors and satin handkerchief holders. We would each buy a nickel's worth of lump milk chocolate at the candy counter to mouth as we

On November Sundays . . . we hunted partridge berries in the pine woods.

trudged from counter to counter, choice to choice. It was exacting and final — taking several afternoons — for the dime stores would not take back or exchange.

Mother made fruitcakes, and for weeks ahead the family picked the nut meats of pecans and walnuts, careful of the bitter layer of the pecans that lined your mouth with nasty fur. At the last I was allowed to blanch the almonds, pinching the scalded nuts so that they sometimes hit the ceiling or bounced across the room. Mother cut slices of citron and crystallized pineapple, figs, and dates, and candied cherries were added whole. We cut rounds of brown paper to line the pans. Usually the cakes were mixed and put into the oven when we were in school. Late in the afternoon the cakes would be finished, wrapped in

A young girl puts the final touches on her turn-of-the-century tree.

white napkins on the breakfast-room table. Later they would be soaked in brandy. These fruitcakes were famous in our town, and Mother gave them often as Christmas gifts. When company came thick slices of fruitcake . . . were always served. When you held a slice of fruitcake to the window or the firelight the slice was translucent, pale citron green and yellow and red, with the glow and richness of our church windows.

Daddy was a jeweler, and his store was kept open until midnight all Christmas week. I, as the eldest child, was allowed to stay up late with Mother until Daddy came home. Mother was always nervous without a "man in

the house." . . . Nothing ever happened on those evenings in Christmas week, but I felt grown, aged suddenly by trust and dignity. Mother confided in secrecy what the younger children were getting from Santa Claus. I knew where the Santa Claus things were hidden, and was appointed to see that my brother and sister did not go into the back-room closet or the wardrobe in our parents' room.

Christmas Eve was the longest day, but it was lined with the glory of tomorrow. The sitting-room smelled of floor wax and the clean, cold odor of the spruce tree. The Christmas tree stood in a corner of the front room, tall as the ceiling, majestic, undecorated. It was our family custom that the tree was not decorated until after we children were in bed on Christmas Eve night. We went to bed very early, as soon as it was winter dark. I lay in the bed beside my sister and tried to keep her awake.

"You want to guess again about your Santa Claus?"

"We've already done that so much," she said.

My sister slept. And there again was another puzzle. How could it be that when she opened her eyes it would be Christmas while I lay awake in the dark for hours and hours?

Christmas Eve was the longest day, but it was lined with the glory of tomorrow.

The time was the same for both of us, and yet not at all the same. What was it? How? I thought of Bethlehem and cherry candy, Jesus and skyrockets. It was dark when I awoke. We were allowed to get up on Christmas at five o'clock. Later I found out that Daddy juggled the clock Christmas Eve so that five o'clock was actually six. Anyway it was always still dark when we rushed in to dress by the kitchen stove. The rule was that we dress and eat breakfast before we could go in to the Christmas tree. On Christmas morning we always had fish roe, bacon and grits for breakfast. I grudged every mouthful for who wanted to fill up on breakfast when there in the sitting-room was candy, at least three whole boxes? After breakfast we lined up, and carols were started. Our voices rose naked and mysterious as we filed through the door to the sitting-room. The carol, unfinished, ended in raw yells of joy.

The Christmas tree glittered in the glorious candlelit room. There were bicycles and bundles wrapped in tissue paper. Our stockings hanging from the mantelpiece bulged with oranges, nuts and smaller presents. The next hours were paradise. The blue dawn at the window brightened, and the candles were blown out. By nine o'clock we had ridden the wheel presents and dressed in the clothes gifts. We visited the neighborhood children and were visited in turn. Our cousins came and grown relatives from distant neighborhoods. All through the morning we ate chocolates. At two or three o'clock the Christmas dinner was served. The dining-room table had been let out with extra leaves and the very best linen was laid—satin damask with a rose design. Daddy asked the blessing, then stood up to carve the turkey. Dressing, rice and giblet gravy were served. There were cut-glass dishes of sparkling jel-lies and stateliness of festal wine. For dessert there was always sillabub or charlotte and fruitcake. The afternoon was almost over when dinner was done.

At twilight I sat on the front steps, jaded by too much pleasure, sick at the stomach and worn out. The boy next door skated down the street in his new Indian suit. A girl spun around on a crackling son-of-a-gun. My brother waved sparklers. Christmas was over. I thought of the monotony of Time ahead, unsolaced by the distant glow of paler festivals, the year that stretched before another Christmas—eternity.

Memory's Door

Old homes, old towns, old friends,
Old ties we all hold dear,
All bind us closer to the past
With every passing year.
The far horizons lure
And beckon us; in youth
We journey forth for fortune, fame,
Or maybe, search for truth.

Old homes, old towns, old friends,
Old ties we all hold dear,
All locked within our memory
Grow dearer every year;
And when we use the key
That opens memory's door,
We see old homes, old towns, old friends
We loved long years before.

Dora P. Fortner

INDEX

Adams, Georgia B. 35
Alcott, Amos Bronson 57
Alcott, Louisa May 148
American Girl 30
Baker, Russell .124
Bandstand in the Park, The 34
Bishop, Henry Rowley 138
Blake, James W. 14
Bohemian Girl, The 46
Bond, Agnes Davenport 61, 79
Bread and Button-Holes 148
Brown-Stocking Easter, A 106
Burn, Paula Zoe 28
Bus of My Own, A 112
Calendar of Childhood, The 130
Campbell, Anne 133
Candy Store, The 12
Cantwell, Mary 30
Carroll, Gladys Hasty 116
Casey Jones 100
Cather, Willa 46
Christmas in the Woods 76
Circus-Day Parade, The 36
Clayton, LaReine Warden 134
Country Doctor, The 68
Country Road, A 45
Country Schoolhouse 67
Crowell, Reid 55
Crumley, Lucille 45
Cudd, Jo 106
Down in the Valley 50
Especially Father 110
Family Cow, The 58
Farewell, My Lovely! 94
Farmer Remembers, A 55
Flecha, Marcos 122
Fortner, Dora P. 159

Foster, Thelma E. 113
Gentle Twilight 43
Gilbreth, Frank B., Jr. 98
Give Me an Old-Fashioned Peddler . . .142
Growing Up 124
Guest, Edgar A. 19, 140
Hayes, Janice Porter 56
Hayman, Carol Bessent 130
Holmes, Marjorie 88, 142
Home for Christmas 156
Home Sweet Home 138
Home Town 8
Hometown Lights 113
Hood, Thomas 115
How Firm a Foundation 22
I Remember, I Remember 115
In a Little World These Men
    Stood Tall .16
Jaques, Edna 64, 73, 84
Lane, The 56
Lawlor, Chas. B. 14
Lebrecht, Donna 34
Lehrer, Jim 112
Little Church, The 19
Lizzie, My Love and You, A 88
McCullers, Carson 156
McGinnis, R. J. 58, 68
McGuire, Marion 40
Memories of Afar 83
Memory, A 133
Memory's Door 159
Middleton, Helen E. 67
Miller, Chas. .14
Mlcuch, Peggy 83
Monnette, Helen 105
Murton, Jessie Wilmore 43
My Hometown 28

Newton, Eddie 100
North Dakota Cook 70
Nostalgia 133
Now, Be a Little Lady 134
Odum, Mamie Ozburn 93
Otten, Catherine 16
Path to Home, The 140
Payne, John Howard 138
Picnic to the Hills, The 84
Prairie Born 73
Pritchard, Glen 37
Railroad, The 102
Remember a Town 7
Remembering .61
Ribbon for Baldy, A 52
Rich, Louise Dickinson 8, 22, 76
Riley, James Whitcomb 36
Rosenteur, Phyllis I. 12
School, The 64
Seibert, T. Lawrence 100
Sidewalks of New York, The 14
Stinson, Sheila .7
Streetlights 40
Strong, Patience 133
Stuart, Jesse 52
Taber, Gladys 110
Thomson, James 107
Time Out for Happiness 98
To Remember Forever 116
Train, The 105
Upon Returning 121
What Became of America's
    Front Porches? 122
White, E. B. 94, 102
White, May Smith 121
Wilde, Oscar .29
Young, Carrie .70

PHOTOGRAPHY CREDITS